From Stage *to* ... Blossoms

Poems and Prose from a Polarized Era

Co-author Nuzhat Alam

Written by Kausam Salam

Art by Sarah Hasan

Educator by career
Writer by necessity
Muslim by choice

Fulton Books
Meadville, PA

Published by Fulton Books 2022

ISBN 979-8-88505-447-8 (paperback)
ISBN 979-8-88731-638-3 (hardcover)
ISBN 979-8-88505-448-5 (digital)

Printed in the United States of America

Contents

1. 9 Minutes and 29 Seconds to Die...1
2. Can We All Not Become Chauvinistic? 3
3. When There Is No Due Process: The Karen in Me.................5
4. Happy Birthday, Leonardo Da Vinci! 8
5. We Will Not Forget Jasper, Texas: Mr. Byrd 10
6. Harsh Graders on Earth Are Harsher than the
    Almighty Himself..13
7. To Make Sense of the World 15
8. Transcending Identities 16
9. There Wasn't a Day...18
10. Rays of Light (That Make Us Work or Think Hard,
    Those Karens)..20
11. In Memory of a Genius Mathematician Colleague/Friend.....22
12. Redbird, Oh Redbird 24
13. She Don't Look Like No English Teachaa........................26
14. Leonardo da Vinci Day 29
15. The Microcosm of the Nation 31
16. Conversational Poem to a Family Member 33
17. For the Firm in Faith: Sister Saboohi, Principal 34
18. Extremism: A Relative Concept...36
19. Countenance Unseen 38
20. The Ballad of Timothy McVeigh, the Bullied Boy.............40
21. Thank You, Allah, for Teaching Me to Suffer 44
22. Recollection from a Team Meeting....................................46
23. Our New Yorker Grandmother...48
24. On Juneteenth Becoming a National Holiday: Prose Poem ...49

25. The War Is Not between Jesus and Muhammad (Peace Be on Them)..53
26. Exhausting Work (As All Therapeutic Works Are) 55
27. Literary Meeting..57
28. When Cancel Culture Turns Lethal, No One Knows............59
29. The Given Well of Our Self-Compassion: El Camino Real....62
30. Conroe, Del Lago: Being in One's Element: A School Academic Retreat under Ms. Sue Pope's Fair Supervision 64
31. Conroe, Del Lago...70
32. Imagine All the Youngest Children....................................72
33. Mango Drink Misplaced and Found 73
34. At the DPS: Microcosm of a Public School with Potential and Tact..75
35. One's Weight in Gold or How We See Ourselves..................78
36. To Be a Mom 80
37. On Your Birthday...82
38. Old Souls and Youth: Twelve Pink Roses Bloom and Fade.....84
39. Critics They Call Vampires Who Know Not What Vampires Are...87
40. Curiosity is the Learners' Way (Alistair Reid): Dystopia's Utopia 90
41. Honorary House Visited in England 92
42. Wasn't Rough Man Created So Impatient? 94
43. On Welcoming President Obama.......................................97
44. Shock of All Shocks...99
45. Those Who Cannot Even Honor the Tortured Man after Death 101
46. Bandwagon 103
47. Nature's Guardians...105
48. The Chasers and the Makers...107
49. The Precious Hummingbird 117
50. Alignment..121
51. Manhattan Rain 123

9 Minutes and 29 Seconds to Die

*The pawn always sits stunned, chained, unable
to move beneath God's magnificent power. //
It is essential for the heart's coronation for the
pawn to realize // there is nothing but Divine
movement in this world [and our God-given
human reason to choose between right conduct
and wrong conduct at every instance].*
—Hafiz, "The Heart's Coronation"

*Discover what it is that gives you pain and
then refuse under any circumstances whatsoever
to inflict that pain onto anybody else.*
—Karen Armstrong

March 29, 2021, 12:12 p.m.

George Floyd's slow death by human hands,
Steeped in animosity, if not pure loathing,
Machine humans who couldn't hear "I can't breathe"
Or "Mama" when any man is desperate.

Ironic that the backdrop of this scene is *Cup Foods: Fresh
Meat and Produce*, where lost boy Derek Chauvin and his silent
        officers
Lived to see their gruesome crime—

Psychopaths (and other humans too) can be like cannibals eating off the feeling flesh of another (if we do not study
ourselves and our good and evil potentials)—
Fresh meats, relishing in sick pleasure of taking life blood in
minutes,
Some, in years, using their prowess and powers to blight the
human.

If the world did not see the blessed video-taker's graphic scene,
this would
Have been just another case where due process was processed,
Shoved under racism's bright rugs, leaving trails of human tears on

America's famous canvas. But those insecure people smile in
their senile ways and, even in some white-collared professions, get increased dopamine in their veins, leak by leak
of violence pouting away, never ashamed.
Let every cannibal feeding on human souls be out in the open
now.
Let every food prey of cannibals be seen by the blind-sighted
public,
Saying loudly, clearly, *"I can't breathe. Please! Mama! I can't
breathe."*

Let every artist paint each surface exactly from her interior,
For the public, hard to please. Out, out. Will those blood-
carved hands
Ever be clean?

Can We All Not Become Chauvinistic?

*May we think of freedom, not as the
right to do as we please, but as the
opportunity to do what is right.*
—Peter Marshall

*It is not possible to complete yourself without
sorrow. Sorrow is a vital ingredient that shapes
the heart and enriches it. So endure sadness the
best you can when its season comes. [Amen.]*
—Hafiz

March 24, 2021

Who says poetry doesn't need to matter and that abstract ideas do nothing concrete for our thoughts?

I have been changed by abstract thoughts written everywhere in
    the world.
People's temperaments can change at the drop of a hat
The jingle of a coin
A mendicant's wish for peaceful living for all people
A mendicant for God, not for man.
Let us not become chauvinistic
As one holding color grudges, caste grudges, workplace grudges
    of insecurity in hardened pockets
For centuries, embodied into one person.

Are we not all be capable of *dividing people into cards?*
Imagine that we are better, so much better, than the ones we have
        underneath our boots, our hands, our fists, and our armies
        of hatred,
Our shouts of jubilation about our own but not the other
Whom we imagine embodies everything we detest about one that
        stands larger than us, fights for his existence, and calls on
        his mother when suffering indecencies that none of us could
        handle if we were hard-pressed like that.
Who says we can't all be George Floyd too *at some point,*
Suffocated to death by the condemning "knees" of a powerful
        one hating on our strength and physical largeness while
Saying, "*I can't breathe. I can't breathe.* Stop, please"?
George died remembering his blessed mother as the whole
World watched his dying slowly.
Some die remembering the One who loves us all much, much
        more than a mother, saying, "I can't breathe." In abstrac-
        tions, our concreteness comes alive:
Some for fire. Some for love. Some for peace inside as well as
        outside.
And not many are martyred for trying to be more powerful than
        the selfish enemy, calling herself/himself an enemy beside
        us,
Tearing the walls of our heart with so much loathing that noth-
        ing moves us anymore.
Those very knees that could be used for prayer are now symbols
        of a stampede upon a heart, and I, at least, do not care for
        more history of where that came from:
Brutality beyond insecurity.
The live man's mother gave testimony that he was a good boy
        with a good heart. Even I cannot understand that love can
        be so blind.

When There Is No Due Process
The Karen in Me

Just this side of Byzantium, the thing about brain dozing off is most productive is mind's essentiality. [Letting kids be creative and free in their thoughts is just as important as imparting all the school's said and unsaid rules on them, from which they are wont to rebel just for fun; thus, giving the gifted and not-perceived-as-gifted equal opportunities to "doze" in their creativity can lead them away from "going astray" from their own good value systems learned in schools and home.]
—Ray Bradbury, *Dandelion Wine*

April 15, 2021

When schools are permitted to let teachers waste their students' time by doing one worksheet after another, schools are wasting their best resources, potentially losing the next inventor, the next scientist discovering a cure for the latest disease, the next artist, the next social problem solver, or the next work-oriented educator.

As Ben Franklin has said, "Boredom is the devil's workshop." When schoolkids are bored to death in schools, they will do many things that their own consciences are not proud of. How many guided worksheets did I learn from in schools and colleges? Zero.

A kid used to joke out loud that he'd tried many pranks on
    teachers
That would work on some people's lack of seeking knowledge.
Sure, kids make pranks. This is as old as history.
When educators make pranks on fellow educators, they try and
    make history, not having grown up yet,
Wondering why their children haven't grown up yet,
Not taking responsibilities seriously.
It's strange when kids can master thoughts that mature adults
    cannot
And how much humans can learn from everyone, anywhere,
Even the lackadaisically inclined pupils who do not wish to
    learn anything
From anyone, relevant to global events.
No wonder those who watch kids turning into adults tolerate
    severe
Discipline problems, especially today, 2021: serial cursing,
    screaming, behavioral issues, apathy, lethargy, and general
    lack of disrespect—
Going smoothly from school gangs to prison pipelines, still
    winking.
So many resort to punishment as a method of trying to get fist-
    fuls of respect, covering up their own polka-dotted track
    records.
Disrespect in the classroom comes from a lack of inner peace,
    a lack of preparation in knowledge and rejoinders, and a
    lack of empathy...
Kids in unruly classrooms have gotten immune to tough teacher
    talk from teachers not versed in what environments kids
    come from. A hardened heart will not lead to gentler
    mannerisms in students, preparing them for family life.
(I am thankful for that 5 percent of teachers, police officers,
    nurses, and health workers who keep any city peaceful
    and free no matter what their race, creed, lifestyle, or past
    suffering, which they do not inflict on others.)

It all seems to start as early as daycare, parents plopping their
toddlers onto laps of people they should not trust with
precious lives.
Smart, neglected toddlers wink at one another for the ludicrous
behavior of double-winking, mature adults
Who overconfidently preach, "Do this, do that and the other,"
Without ever doing this or that themselves. Kids see through
that.

Manipulation is learned from toddler ages. Some adults don't
outgrow manipulation as this is how they were raised. *What kinds
of people punish unusual* others for their own sinful behaviors and
insecurities?

Last time I checked, scapegoating never made a pleasant society.
How things work where due process isn't normal, where equality is selective, and no teacher is born saying, yay! I want to be the
next activist for society's movements—twenty-six years of service,
yay!
We can either walk away free, hurt, and easy
Or walk out like Kim Potter, screaming, cursing at herself,
Without empathy for life taken in mindlessness, stuck in yet
another prison scene
That could have been avoided due to certain knowledge and
curiosity about how diverse people will behave and react based on
what baggage they already carry,
Forgiving no ingenue patience, peace, and dignity.
*Let them laugh at you and mock you, oh people of diverse creeds
and ways of being. Let them call you insulting names. It's they, not you,
who shall invite their raging selves to inner prison once again.*

Happy Birthday, Leonardo Da Vinci!

*O mankind! We created you from a single pair of
a male and a female and made you into Nations
and Tribes—that you may know each other,
not that you may despise each other. Verily, the
most honored of you in the sight of Allah is he
who is the most righteous of you. And Allah has
full knowledge and is well-acquainted with all
things. The desert Arabs say, "We believe." Say,
"You have no faith;" but you only say, "We have
submitted our wills to Allah," for Faith has not yet
entered your hearts. But if you obey Allah and His
Messenger, He will not belittle anything of your
deeds: for Allah is Oft-Forgiving, Most Merciful.*
          —Sura 49, "The Inner Apartments"

April 15, 2021

In crowded rooms of suspicion, I felt alone;
The world's thick sorrows came upon me, and I felt alone.
This cold world of empty optimism and braggadocio
Where evil sometimes acts like good and good is treated evil,
Where doing right by the Lord's commands

Is wrong to certain people, and still, one feels alone, framed but
          freed,
Where drugs, liquor, and gender are misused
In place of human trust, and vanity produces unseeing hearts,

A small redbird nestles itself amid the tangled branches as if to
    remind me that it needs no human intervention for its
    sustenance,
Trying very little after its own flight and suffering.
Since then, many redbirds appear and rest near me,
Offering hope and comfort of other beings on earth beside
    ourselves,
Where any seeing eye may watch while walking.

And how You set it forward is beyond imagination—how you
    turn
Our lives around when we get stuck somewhere,
Lightening the human heart with strength when grief s it was,
Giving comfort, conscience, and peaceful ease for each time I
    gave my trust,
And how you've sheltered me when I was beyond repair.
Ameen.

We Will Not Forget Jasper, Texas
Mr. Byrd

*Among His Signs is this, that He created
you from dust; and then—behold, you
are men scattered far and wide!*
    —Sura 30

*Say, O People of the Book! You have no ground
to stand upon unless you stand fast by the Law,
the Gospel, and all the Revelation that has
come to you from your Lord…will you worship,
besides God, something which has no power
either to harm or benefit you?… O People of the
Book! Exceed not in your religion the bounds
of what is proper, trespassing beyond truth,
nor follow the vain desires of people who went
wrong in times gone by, who misled many,
and strayed themselves from the even Way.*
    —Sura 5

*And do not swell your cheek for pride at men,
nor walk in insolence through the earth; for
Allah does not love any arrogant boaster.*
    —Sura 31

April 15, 2021

Never forget Jasper, Texas, as Mr. Byrd was made to fall.

I cannot forget Mr. Byrd's face
Dragged across the road
To his death
Only due to his race

A foreshadowing of
George Floyd's death from
Many years earlier
Some will say that was not about race

A dragging death
Of anyone is the worst in the human race
How dare we judge and kill another
To "relieve" our inner rage?

But just as rotten as dragging men
Or women to their death or crucifying them
As Herod planned—as generalizing
Tribes of humans into (either) good or evil

As if we were deities ourselves,
And God were not judging between
His tribes' individual deeds—
How we degrade our human
Brother is how we degrade God Himself.

Today I read about a Pakistani American man, Mr. Mohammed
Anwar, a liber worker, who was made to be dragged and die at the
hands of two unruly, unusually cruel fourteen-year-olds. Imagine
that. After his tortured death, the two African American teens will be
tried as adults. When people are heedless and have no care for peo-

ple's lives, entire societies are transformed into something we cannot describe. May Allah give peace eternally to the martyrs of any violence and to their families too. Ameen.

Harsh Graders on Earth Are Harsher than the Almighty Himself

April 15, 2021

Here are other versions of the aphorism "Excessive pride is the downfall of humankind."

> We have sent you, O men, a Messenger, to a witness concerning you, even as We sent a Messenger to Pharaoh. // But Pharaoh disobeyed the Messenger, so We seized him with a heavy punishment. [Some Quranic interpreters have noted that prideful and arrogant Pharaoh remembered God Almighty when it was too late, and therefore, posterity used him as a model for extreme arrogance while drowning.] (Sura 73)

> You serve as an example to others by sacrificing the ego and accepting the guidance of the Higher Power. (*I Ching*)

> If you love me, you will keep my commands. [All of them implied]. And I will ask the Father, and he will give you another Counselor to be with you forever. He is the Spirit of Truth. The world is unable to receive him because it doesn't see him or know him. But you do know him, because he remains with you and will be in

you…the Counselor, the Holy Spirit, whom the
Father will send in my name, will teach you all
things and remind you of everything I have told
you. (John 14:15)

Some rush to be great people
Without treating people good enough—
Putting on one face here
And another few faces there.

We humans here
On this plane want to shine,
Shine, shine without first being dim
Or dumb enough in numbness,
Submitting to the Divine.

To shells by the seashore,
Deeply listening—
Sometimes doing nothing *is* doing something.
So I let go of dogmas and confusions
And follow logical intuition,
Where I am no more
Than an atom submitting to the One.

Some save face near Grandma,
Some near mosque or church.
Some brave faces at an interview
Dim their inner light from God,
Who sees all we say and do
When no one sees us,
Or false advertisement companies
Pretending to do no harm
To everyone who counts
In making the world a better place to be.

To Make Sense of the World

Those who are steadfastly balanced,
humble, and in harmony with the Sage
inherit everything under the sun.
—I Ching

Give measure and weight with full justice;
no burden do We place on any soul, but that
which it can bear; whenever you speak, speak
justly, speak justly even if a near relative is
concerned; and fulfil the Covenant of Allah.
—Sura Ananv

April 14, 2021

To make sense of the world, Da Vinci
Studied everything, especially himself…
Long, long hours that may seem useless
To anybody else, Da Vinci dedicated to
Exploration, asked the major questions
We ask at some point when ready to
Venture into the blue beyond: who, what,
Why, how, where, what for, what is my role, etc.
Where is that love for learning today
So that we are more than our ambitions and wallet sizes,
Having room to play with life just enough
To understand how we are made?

Transcending Identities

In their effort to divorce language and experience,
deconstructionist critics remind me of middle-
class parents who do not allow their children
to play in the streets. [Excessive rebellion at
home begins when parents say no to everything
or when teachers resent children or "lesser"
teachers; being themselves at all times while
donning personality masks are the norm.]
—Jacques Derrida

A discerning mind seeks knowledge, but
the mouth of fools feeds on foolishness.
—Proverbs 15:14

Better to be lowly of spirit with the humble
than to divide plunder with the proud.
—Proverbs 16:19

First, the monarch butterfly in morn's landing visits briefly on
the porch pathway—
Exchanges, then the swallowtail butterfly, lingering on the
leaves,
A divine gift of healing after years of discomfort during
walking—
My normal activity since toddlerhood;
God has a way of making human curiosities normal
While humans have a way of making the abnormal seem normal.

As butterflies dance in the natural cosmos, so do we align with nature and move to the rhythm we have within.

No need for the music of discord, screeching sounds of people who crave noise ceaselessly to erase their pains inside (until the next trauma happens, perplexing them).

God's glorious nature frees the spirit from the combustive engines of people wrought with painful differences they've learned to present before themselves, and butterflies that remain near flowers growing for so long remind me of that freedom. That freedom is meant to be freed.

To be as they are, unconscious in their consciousness of being where they are, despite all odds.

(And sure, there are scores of people collecting butterflies in jars like pretty scars or bells and whistles, signaling to people how and who they are,

But butterflies simply move to their imperturbable beat,

Lingering for a time, exploring a sweet terrain, then fleeting for their comfort elsewhere to have a go at life again.)

Ameen.

There Wasn't a Day

*I am a part of all that I have met: yet all
experience is an arch where-through / gleams
that untraveled world whose margin fades
/ forever and forever when I move.*
                        —Alfred, Lord Tennyson

July 7, 2021

There wasn't a day in teaching when I wasn't quite content
Each day, I'd wanted to make a comfort zone for all my students
No matter how many of them—sometimes forty in a classroom—
A sanctuary away from their lives' brouhaha so they'd chance to
     mend
Themselves, learning through thought discipline,
Understanding their purposes, the goals they'd make,
So that they, too, would always be content in career and family
     choices
Without regret.

But every few years, downstairs would call me in to testify if
anything had been accomplished after all, so I'd have to play the role
of my own quiet lawyer in a system where learning wasn't supposed
to bring enthusiasm at all or freedom of choice in readings within the
curriculum, my number one.

I wouldn't trade back those years, twenty-six or so, nor any student I'd ever taught, (except the few brainwashed to think like fear-
mongers, who couldn't stand to see ones so content in learning's environment). Why not remove the learning ones from contentment,

where higher learning and soul-searching while writing never really mattered much at all?

> Still, when the learners would surprise me by how much they
>> wrote, hundreds of pages per semester, dozens of books
>> they'd read on their own,
> Scholarships from places I had not imagined, I knew that teach-
>> ing would always be my calling regardless of what down-
>> stairs thought of me and my world.

> We are not now that strength which in old
> days /moved earth and heaven, that which we are,
> we are— / one equal temper of heroic hearts, //
> made weak by time and fate, but strong in will/to
> strive, to seek, to find, and not to yield. (Alfred,
> Lord Tennyson, for whom success was also bad
> at times, may Allah bless his calling and works.
> Ameen.)

Rays of Light
(That Make Us Work or Think Hard, Those Karens)

And Allah advances those in guidance who seek
guidance: and the things that endure, Good
Deeds, are best in the sight of your Lord, as
rewards, and best of their eventual returns.
—Sura Mary 19:76

June 19, 2021

My fourth-grade friend was named Karen. She was blind, but she saw more clearly than us with a vision blessed. She could see through the troubled kids.

She would get a lunch ice cream for those who had no dessert. I was one of them, rich enough in spirit but not rich enough for desserts every day.

She was from a poor family but had a heart as large as the sea.

Teachers, as smart as they were in the New York elementary school, placed her in sheltered positions, mollycoddling her, but Karen had the perfect words for every question and the hardest work ethic in the fourth grade.

As her name says, *"ray of light, hard work ethic."* It is a Germanic name with a biblical meaning.

Karen, in Mr. Becker's class, defended the rights of playground children from the bully, MJ's, unexpected bouts of violence, standing up to unreasonable people. We need those rays of light like Karen in our lives.

Friends may live in our lives for so long, as directed by the Highest Director, but still they leave an indelible mark on each of us.

Who knows what name meanings may do for the richness of a child's personality? Unless we get to the root of things by naming them if we can.

Who knows how many Karens out there are doing something that no one ever dared to think of doing before—making sense out of nonsense or bringing to light something new that we haven't thought of before?

In Memory of a Genius Mathematician Colleague/Friend

*There never was a truly great man that was
not at the same time truly virtuous.*
—Benjamin Franklin

Study the past, if you would divine the future.
—Confucius (one of the first of the
ancients who taught the Golden Rule
before we knew what it was)

April 14, 2021

If Mr. David Hallmark were here on earth to see today's plight,
(*Can you hear me up there, Mr. Hallmark?*)
I'm certain he'd wear blue, not red, and care for all people's
    well-being,
As he always did and said.
He should have been at least a team leader, a motivational
    speaker,
Or a superintendent in a certain regimented school
With thousands of narrative pages of Kansas wisdom to his
    credit, giving his people the loving name that they deserve.
Someday, I shall see those pages come to life,
Filled with the joyous beauty of Kansas life.
But no. Dave Hallmark was a true teacher at heart, just like me.
    He kept amusing people with mathematical analogies,
Dream schemes, and character analyses, just like me,

Talking gently and bemusedly, overthinking almost everything,
    just like me.
But I was a dark-brown, foreign-seeming Muslim female among
    that despot crowd of leaders hard-knuckled, embracing
    buttering narcissists everywhere,
And I was just as much as a blunt whistleblower when wrong
    things were done before my eyes anywhere.
For David, respect and trust went far with him,
A being gracefully made by merciful God:
Anything goes in his class, where everyone equally cared.
For Kausam, even her name was mispronounced on purpose,
Her race and creed belittled since the beginning when Hopper
And Worthy left—except for her true family and students who
    knew her
Heart and mind's true intentions. Yet nothing good of her could
    ever be said by the party of status.
Perhaps in heaven, we get another chance with striving.
One of His seven heavens, as He has forecast,
Where people true to His laws have team meetings too,
Meeting soul family members unreservedly that here on earth
    could not succeed;
In that throne above the skies where divergent paths of good-
    ness meet in class and creed, loving God Almighty nearer
    to us than our veins.

Redbird, Oh Redbird

Every soul will be held in pledge for its deeds.
　　　　　—Sura "The One Wrapped Up"

If a person is living out his Personal Legend,
he knows everything he needs to know.
There is only one thing that makes a dream
impossible to achieve: the fear of failure.
　　　　　　　　　　—Paulo Coelho

You serve as an example by giving up your ego
and accepting the guidance of the Higher Power.
　　　　　　　　　　　—I Ching

Don't testily against your neighbor without
cause. Don't deceive with your lips. Don't
say, "I'll do to him what he did to me."
　　　　　　　　—Proverbs 24:28–29

Those who love to see scandal published,
broadcast among the Believers, will have a
grievous Penalty in this life and the Hereafter:
Allah knows, and you do not know.
　　　　　　　—Sura 24, "The Light"

June 18, 2021

Redbird, oh redbird,
You walk on man's instruments.
How do you balance on small, sacred feet?
Only by instinct God gave me, you see.
Redbird, oh redbird,
How seem you so happy?
I take what God gives me, and so I am freed
From taking, looting, hoarding, piling, or grabbing.
O redbird, redbird, you seem heaven-sent.
Are you a spirit of my father/mother now absent?
You shall know someday, but now you're not ready.
Study your scriptures with caution and joy.
Live as your last day; live unburdened each day.
Redbird, oh redbird, each phase, I have seen you and your
    blessed family too
Between men's caged fences and human boundaries, each of my
    traumas, four seasons as Vivaldi.
Who knows, noble human, but the Maker on how you shall be.
    Just balance for Allah, clothed in dignity.
[It seems only a redbird, but the redbird is free
From humans' desperate sinning or slave-meanderings toward
    objects of worship requiring too much need.
Rather, redbirds fly high, coming to earth when they want
On wings that are free,
On souls that are freed, light, and easy.
Ameen.]

She Don't Look Like No English Teachaa

*[The Priest] didn't talk to me about God anymore,
and I never saw him as worked up as he was that
first day…a few questions, a brief conversation
with my lawyer, and the examinations were over.*
—Albert Camus, *The Stranger*

*Marie said it was terrible that I didn't
say anything. She asked me to go find a
policeman, but I told her I didn't like cops.*
—Meursault, *The Stranger*

*The day of my arrest I was first put in a room
where there were already several other prisoners,
most of them Arabs. They laughed when they
saw me. They asked me what I was in for. I said
I'd killed an Arab and they were all silent.*
—Meursault, *The Stranger*

*Don't crush the oppressed at the city gate, for
the Lord will champion their cause. [Today,
Meursault is a common personality trait.]*
—Proverbs)

April 14, 2021

Said the pimple-faced, ruddy, raging new assistant with an agenda bigger than his shoulders. Chaucer, the thinkers' literary father, would say, "People do look like their character from time to time."

Well, that one, the new assistant, hadn't read much Chaucer or anything else, by the actions and gestures I should not have observed as he made his rounds. (I hope he changes for his kids, if not for God.)

"Watchoo mean by that, man! She been teachin' here since the second year. This building began when old George Hopper was in charge, wearing his light-up green sneakers in the stadium, where he knew each student's name and teacher by heart!

"Just makes me so sad, man, that beeches we be fightin' to kill off was gonna look like that. She ain't no fuckin' English teachaa like my matron. Folks be teaching English down and up this town since time began.

"But see, my man, anybody can know any subject. It don't have to be like what they look like, their darn skin tone, or their background," said the wise, old echo of Mr. Zimmerman, who could have taught all of them a thing or two, ready, so ready, to retire from a place that went from earth's heaven to Rome's eggshells.

"Well, so," said the new *assi*stant, belly sticking out of his beer madness due to his wifey's henpecked suppression as a Klansman type, not getting enough from his stingy, pretty-no-time-for-her, extra-feminist desire to acquire things and outdo him. "Be sure bettin' on it that the Mosleeem beeches, Black beetches, Chinese beetches, and even that French doctorate beetch don't be teachin' no humanities stuff around me. We be needin' moe readin', mathematik, and a little bit of writin'. I be failin' them skinny subjects when the real English teachaas be gradin' me for tryin' harder to succeed in them stupid-ass classes. Now I got somewhere. See? I gots connections and am gonna go get 'em all and grab some 'em by the pussy and arms and such, like our guy told us we could do to them loud, thinkin' women!"

"Shoot. You think you got it all figured out," said the wise Zimmerman's voice, dangling around the petty man's ears. "Since when do classes get stupid asses? You need to watch what you say around here. We have got to be more fair around here in evaluating teachers in George Hopper-founded beacon school before your types min it.

"Yeah, yeah, be tryin'. I like them A and M blondes teachin' up here and them brunettes teachin' English 'cuz they be easy on the eyes and going to my clubs after work, and some of them be so open and fine. Ya know what I mean? They be openin' all kinds of windows and doors for us henpecked,

tight-fisted husbands. It's not even damn funny. Up there in I-rakk and Afganistaano, we be having to rape some of them wise beetches, as my novelist buddy knows, comin' down here for sho'. It's kinda charitable, ya know? Now don't you be tellin' my little two-year-old what kinds of things I be doin' on the side of this here job!"

"No need. The kids will find out way before you try hiding anything from them. I'd change my ways if I were you, young man," said the real assistant principal who had read John in the Bible.

Leonardo da Vinci Day

*"The wolf and the lamb will feed together, and
the lion will eat straw like cattle, but the serpent's
food will be dust! They will not do what is evil or
destroy on my entire holy mountain," says the Lord.*
—Isaiah

*I have come to gather all nations and
languages: they will come and see my glory. I
will establish a sign among them, and I will
send survivors from them to the nations.*
—Isaiah 66:18–19

*[God knew that the Roman Empire would at first
be victorious, as historical tables keep changing;
scholars, please check your sources as I only know
this from intuition.] And among His Signs is
the creation of the Heavens and the earth, and
the variations in your languages and your colors:
verily in that are Signs for those who know.*
—Sura "The Roman Empire"

*To you We sent the Scripture confirming the
Scripture that came before it, and guarding it in
safety… We have prescribed a Law and an Open
Way. If Allah had so willed, He would have made
you a single people, but His Plan is to test you in*

> *what He has given you, so strive as in a race in all*
> *virtues. [What a precious gift is our free will.]*
> —Sura "The Table Spread"

April 15, 2021

Today, this brilliant, cloudy fresco day,
Reminds me of Leonardo da Vinci's birthday
On April 15—
When the moist, green earth and thick, wide trees
May paint themselves onto a church fresco scene.

As Leonardo painted what he saw
And what was in his heart of hearts,
So may we go back to painting what our
Eyes have seen, not just others' words
Spoken for heard meanings.

The Microcosm of the Nation

Cling to the power of higher truth.
—I Ching

Such as took their religion to be mere amusement
and play, and were deceived by the life of the
world. That day we shall forget them as they
forgot the meeting of this day of theirs, (with their
Lord), and as they were wont to reject Our Signs.
—Sura 7 "The Heights"

Do not make your deeds vain.
—Sura 47, "The Prophets"

May 7, 2021

It was a microcosm of coldness in the macrocosm of national stiffness.

Uppity tones after suicides? "Something good will come of these, see? Something really bright and good" (as if a few cakes had burned in her oven only).

The rest of us had to succor the learners' hearts as they were drowning in their friends' sorrows, letting student leaders go and offer consolation.

Genuine.

Instead of letting academics go on at that time of chaos as if nothing major happened, what if it were them? What if they felt homes' losses? Such uppity leaders never think like that. They'd only learned how to skin their cats.

Stiffness. Coldness can get us rich jobs but not much else.

As our high school biology coach, Mr. Roache, would say, "Guys, only dissect the cat, pig, or frog if you're used to not feeling much at all. Otherwise, let the lab partner do the job while yous guys do the written report." Now, that Mr. Roache was a sensitive teacher. I forgot much of what he taught but never forgot that he made me feel important in my skin.

Nowadays, thirty years later, stiffness is a common trend.

Coldness turns the dollars into gold.

Until some good ones give up on life itself, for cold stiffness only means the old age young, emotions going icy, stiffened, and cold.

Conversational Poem to a Family Member

He is the One Who sends to His servants
manifest Signs, that He may lead you from
the depths of darkness into the Light.
　　　　　—Sura Hadid, "The Iron"

July 4, 2018

Nothing like an early morning walk
To sort out night's darker days,
As every cloud's downpour
Brings the sun's resilience.

Each argument in excess, when restrained,
Shows rainbows' silver linings,
For it's not humans alone who will change
But One who quiets our pains.

How many breaks in each fine day
Bring pausing to fruition,
Freeing this heavy soul from overthinking?
Nothing like early morning's rising

To remind myself there's more
On earthly planes and heavenly ones,
Though sulking ones stay sore.
Ameen.

For the Firm in Faith
Sister Saboohi, Principal

*Doors where my heart was used to beat / so quickly,
not as one that weeps / I come once more; the
city sleeps; I smell the meadow in the street... /
But in my spirit will I dwell, / and dream my
dream, and hold it true; / for though my lips may
breathe adieu, / I cannot think a thing farewell.*
—Alfred, Lord Tennyson

March 6, 2021

You took me in when I felt low,
No show of pride, no fear of woe
Where love for all is common sense
Where justice for all: strict due process
Allah's Prophet has been your guide,
Those who love all humankind
No need for a sameness of temperament
No need for braggadocio's indifference
I thought I knew all about democracy
In schools where teachers lead the way
You let me see a pathway straight, exemplified
Where secular realms meet interfaith
Where thinkers who lead and learn remain
Ourselves—no masks inside facial masks
Beige, White, Black, brown, East Coast, south, or
West, eclectic, overworked, or overwhelmed

Your tough-love style, gentle-dressed,
Earned ethics that *each scholar counts*
In vibrant duas for love renowned
Where kindness reigns, no extravagance
May Allah keep you filled with holy
Vibes in teaching teachers hard-earned ethics
Where each soul counts in Masjid Bilal
Where love for all is common sense
For Allah's sake, in justice divine
Ameen

Extremism
A Relative Concept

*When shall we see a life full of steady enthusiasm,
walking straight to its aim, flying home, as that
bird is now, against the wind—with the calmness
and the confidence of one who knows the laws
of God and can apply them? When shall we see
a woman making a study of what she does?*
—Florence Nightingale,
The Woman Question

July 5, 2021

At times, society seems all about whiteness and blackness,
Gayness and nongayness, the female and the male,
As if everything in life should revolve around these concepts
(mostly).
Those who talk with God-consciousness often wonder how
superficial we have become
Or how we are doing in terms of advancing our thought
civilizations.
Some seem to think that thinking itself begins and ends with
race and gender,
Two subjects only. This is progress for many people: dissecting
the colors of one's changing skins, miscegenation in the
southern divisions, or mixing in the nation,
How people choose to embrace someone inside or outside of
their marriages,

Knowing the results beforehand,

And how some have come to despise even marriages, the colors of their skins, or their own families as if a fad is talking to them, blaming the god they say they'd like to believe in

For men's atrocities and women's indecencies having gone so far. No one understands how to study the self anymore to solve issues beyond raging testosterone...before they get out of control.

I wonder how such *extremists in thought, with their black-and-white thinking,* can even teach or learn beyond their exterior selves,

The colors of skin, the politics of race, what will offend, and what shall efface them

So that they may keep importance and take precedence as high matter

Beyond the millions of topics that matter.

Countenance Unseen

You have heard about God being
indivisible; is that just a rumor?

—Hafiz

June 28, 2021

Since Allah is to speak to, pray to is no male god
Nor centered on male deities,
He, the Blessed One, sees how women see, His Rahma/
    compassion
So blessed in ubiquity—the one with an imaginative womb—
Creating existence that shines too brightly that we cannot see
How can God Almighty, I wonder, make us in His image for
    what
Mortal men have done, what they do not yet know?
In soccer fields (today), they move a player quickly,
Better than the one they did replace. How faulty human judg-
    ment is
That it thinks they are like Mt. Olympus deities, bringing ones
    like Hercules,
Who die sooner than they are newly born, making their ways
    onto golden thrones.
But my Allah (the Unseen) is like no other that I have studied
    long and hard
In this rough world of bitterness and part joy, where good-be-
    having ones always are downtrodden by patronizing, hid-
    den codes.

But Mercy, like a true mother's heart, always sees and always
    knows
That God—invisible, indivisible—alone brings justice to us all
    in the USA or elsewhere I have enjoyed. He halts war
    cries in excess, changing poverty when we obey
And that He alone gives from His faculties. Though grateful
    prayers few shall say,
Those inward, seeing faculties, we bring back to Him from daily
    works,
Purifying ourselves for His sake alone.
Amen.

The Ballad of Timothy McVeigh, the Bullied Boy

The wicked are those who rebel against the light. They do not recognize its ways or stay on its paths. The murderer rises at dawn to kill the poor and needy, and by night becomes a thief. The adulterer's eye watches for twilight, thinking, "No eye will see me."
—John 24:13–15

Every man's fate We have fastened to his own neck…who receives Guidance, receives it for his own benefit: who goes astray does so to his own loss: no bearer of burdens can bear the burden of another: nor would We visit with Our Wrath until We had sent a Messenger to give warning.
—Sura 17, "The Israelites"

Do no mischief on the earth, after it has been set in order, but call on Him with fear and longing in your hearts: for the Mercy of Allah is always near to those who do good. [Amen.]
—Sura 7, "The Heights"

Seek union with others and with the Sage.
—I Ching

May 9, 2021

Timothy McVeigh was a bullied boy, a bullied man, so bullied
    at school, at home, in a free country—bullied so much,
    imprisoned in his mind with no moral support.
So he filled his impulse with vitriol, blowing up guns and oth-
    ers' heads,
Blew up his rage on unexpected ones—revenge on anyone walk-
    ing around.
Did he turn to friends? He had one just like him—also blew up
    his tempers upon—
Blew up his tempers upon some "enemy" state that did nothing
    for him,
And did such identify with the braggarts of rank? Timothy
    McVeigh and his lost old friend?
Did Tim McVeigh become Kool Klandestine? For a while, but
    even they gave no succor for a bullied man wrung from
    the inside out right from the home of freed bondsmen.
Was he taught to love?
Was he taught to respect women as a whole and not in parts?
Was he taught respect where respect is lacking?
Was he taught to let go of grudges lurking deep inside his brain?
Was he taught a universally sane sense of ethics and justice for
    all?
If not through God, through society, then? If God, through
    pious regularity, then?
God, who gives justice to everyone in his-'er own due time
And peace if we can handle His wording.
No, Timothy McVeigh did join the army without following
    rules.
This isn't talked about much.
They'd rather talk of the veiled ones and those in turbans and
    such,
The ones who pray at airports for peace for the people,
Peace for themselves through the Almighty's power.

They'd rather assassinate the ones who don't look like good old
    boy Timothy McVeigh.

They'd rather send drones and mobs toward those who don't
    smell like Timothy McVeigh, who may not have bathed
    for days.

Timothy McVeigh, a lost old boy, couldn't hold his penis in his
    camouflage pants,

Who couldn't think kindly of women or men, who couldn't
    hold doors open in decent ways, who couldn't say amen.

As Macbeth and Lady Macbeth, taking the lives of innocent
    civilians,

Even those who looked like them way, way before 9-11.

I have met some potential Timothy McVeighs who profile
    others unusual to them, as I have met the opposite of
    Timothy McVeigh, who take a sour person and turn than
    into gold again.

Of this present time, roaming the streets without butter, bread,
    mothers, or friends, without lived ethics or God's gra-
    cious light,

Who have been minions to Big-Onions, setting up gangs in
    students' parades,

Who knows when the snobbishly high and local mighty open
    their eyes

And their stingy hearts to the Timothy McVeighs still going
    around,

Footloose and fancy-free, ready to kill, maim, or bomb anyone
    not thinking like them, or them, or us, or us in the good
    ole freedom-loving, freedom-losing US of A.

Don't be scared of the Timothy McVeighs; they'll only do what
    is fated for them.

Unless they are taught to see all of people, not parts of people—

Them, us, or you, anyone at all, for Timothy McVeighs come
    from all different veins, all different creeds, and no creeds
    alike, calling themselves high-pride names like rebels and
    such, coming from all different races and classes made by
    man, not God. They stand in vague corners, looking for

someone, anyone with a heart left over. Desperate, lost young ones with no inner peace, harming unarmed civilians who haven't much rage,
Who have vulnerabilities or no jobs at all in a free-living, freedom-loving state of all states.
Do Timothy McVeighs celebrate Mother's Day?
Only for show, if at all.
Do they feed off, mooch off, from their friends' hate more so?
Most probably.

Thank You, Allah, for Teaching Me to Suffer

*Let the peoples praise you, God; let all the
peoples praise you. Let the nations rejoice
and shout for joy, for you judge the peoples
with fairness and lead the nations on earth.
Selah. Let the people praise you, God.*
—Psalm 67

*Those to whom We sent the Book before this,
they do believe in this Revelation...twice will
they be given their reward, (InshAllah) for that
they have persevered, that they avert Evil with
Good, and that they spend in charity out of what
We have given them. And when they hear vain
talk, they turn away therefrom and say: To us
our deeds, and to you, yours; Peace be on you;
we do not seek ignorant (ways). [Amen. It is
often best to walk away when we observe harm
being done (systemically) to ourselves and anyone
else after we had tried and tried to make things
better. If we continue working or residing in
most destructive situations, we have lost respect
for ourselves and may be verging on sadism—an
unhealthy habit even for people who practice this.]*
—Sura 28, "The Narration"

May 7, 2021

Thank you, Allah, for testing me widely while teaching
(Even in years when I hadn't read much from you)
For letting me choose life over other possibilities
For teaching me justice for all and not selective piety
For keeping me away from joining violent groups
Who win temporarily for greed of money
Thank you, Allah, for letting me still believe in peace
After showing me the two highways of which you speak,
Where each has been given mental faculties
Of free will to do good deeds or break loose and live fancy-free
So that we don't get imprisoned by our own vanities,
Gained by thinking we deserve everything
For everything was a gift for us from You.
Summa Ameen.

O ye who believe! Be steadfast witnesses
for Allah in equity, and let not the hatred of any
people seduce you that ye deal not justly. Deal
justly, that is nearer to your duty. Observe your
duty to Allah. Fo! Allah is informed of what ye
do. (Koran, translated by Marmeduke Pickthall,
England)

Recollection from a Team Meeting

*O humankind! We created you from a single
pair of a male and a female, and made you into
nations and tribes, that you may know each other,
not that you may despise each other. Verily, the
most honored of you in the sight of God is he who
is the most righteous of you. And Allah has full
knowledge and is well-acquainted with all things.*
—Sura 49, "The Inner Apartments"

*Superstition sets the whole world in
flames; philosophy quenches them.*
—Voltaire

May 31, 2020

"My husband kills women who *look and think like her*," whispered the young English teacher as I walked into a school
meeting.
She stared at my body, looking up and down, down and up,
from my long skirts to my silent frown.
Her language showed me what some soldiers' wives' lives were
like:
Meager in love, meager in compassion, meager in passion, meager in the force of calm. So up and down the stoned,
pretty eyes went, thinking they could knock me down,
But for my thick skin, absorbing everything, and heavy weight,
And with a million deeds for God's sake that she knew nothing
of, I stood upright

(Supported by two devoted African American leaders who must
    have been there at some point).

"Someday I'll get my PhD," said the ambitious lady, half scorn-
    ing me,

Half admiring me, staring at the few items near my desk in the
    new building.

Up and down, down and up, she'd look at the face of a much
    older person, older in spirit than she'd ever like to be.

And after our talks, counseling-style sessions, coffee, and treats
    when she needed kindness and after all the exchanges
    about her mother's meanness toward her life,

The eager beaver in ambition's tightwad reign pulled and pulled
    her tug-of-war strings, only to find she wasn't climbing
    high enough for them,

And she became dopey and sad again with all the smoke she
    used to take in.

Our New Yorker Grandmother

War is not an adventure. It is a
disease. It is like typhus.
　　　　　　　　—Antoine de Saint Exupéry

2007

Mrs. Sarah Levy—we called her our Jewish grandmother, though Abunnisa Imam and Hameda Khatoon were our grandmothers in India. Her sweet heart met my parents' hearts when we moved from Chicago to New York, finding her while shopping in her long, modest dresses and crimson turban (ladies' style), as we settled down.

She'd visit us in apartment 308 with lots of gifts and love to share.

Then Akka would escort her back down Maple Avenue with that silver walking stroller women carried as she was in her eighties now.

From Kissena Boulevard back to Maple and so on, helping her with groceries near and far, her elder lawyer boy and younger someone important were too busy for their lovely mother, but Sarah Levy was everything we could ever ask for in another grandmother.

It was as if Allah ordained for us all to meet and sit together during meals with loving Uncle. It was never clear who was the panacea for whom in those days, Mrs. Levy or us, when times got rougher. And when Ammi went in for a grueling women's surgery, with special relatives, there sat Sarah Levy, epitomizing all in love, care, and beauty. And it didn't matter that she was a Hassidic Jew and we, Semitic-Indo Muslims in New York. For that same Creator gave us loving healing. Ameen

On Juneteenth
Becoming a National Holiday
Prose Poem

The simple truth is that every moment in
every person's life contains the teaching
he or she most needs at that time.
                                   —*I Ching*

People honor me with their lips, but their
heart is far from me. They worship me in vain,
teaching as doctrines human commands.
                          —Matthew 15:8–9

There are among us some that are righteous, and
some the contrary: we follow divergent paths.
                          —Sura 72, "The Spirits"

June 19, 2021

By the grace of justice, by the joy of equality, through people
who mean well, it took centuries for civil citizens of educated folks
to realize how much the American slaves had suffered in the land of
the freed.

Is this the politics of belonging? Does this not belong in some
school where children are freed?

Or shall we use the pretext of crushes and love in place of what
really matters in schools today—justice and equal treatment of all

its people? The American slaves freed into free people deserved that same treatment in Tulsa, Oklahoma. But things are changing for many people. Things are changing because educated people are seeing the bigger picture instead of bigots in the picture.

Centuries it took for all of us to realize how much the American freed peoples will no longer be slaves to an antiquated system still practiced by unfair people across the world. Why would holy God answer our prayers if we live in such a system where success is destroyed due to perverse reasons?

"Oh, they were freed already! They were freed!"

Still, they were not freed, our brothers and sisters, still not freed.

Though, successfully they made their marks too on society.

Building their own freedom after years of slavery for generations—did that not affect years of future generations in the cycle of poverty, giving them a lack of confidence?

Burned down for vanity's deception through Satan's deception!

And when we, the universal we anywhere in the bright cosmos, were made to suffer for things we believed in and for people we believed in, working crazy hard to be good and decent in career and family for a nation we loved with all of our heart for the sake of Allah before any flag or nationalistic warring, why, why were we made to suffer deeply?

No rich person's so-sorry money could compensate for the national ancestors' suffering anywhere—not in this land, not elsewhere.

No devotee of Christ Himself could understand his (expected) crucifixion at the hands of raging mobs, depending on which side of any religious wall we look on from.

Now America is looking more like the America I knew and loved in the eighties. I even bought a freedom candle to commemorate the national holiday for our brothers and sisters. Let that light shine through that America where people might speak freely or defend fellow women who are being trespassed upon by hoodlums dressed in authority badges of control for no justifiable reasons but their bloodlust—except that they are (only) men and not deities and women who blindly follow (only) men, not seekers of God or truth of any kind.

No, I can't imagine the feeling of having information on what my ancestors had done (if they hadn't been free) or what fields they were beaten on with whipping sticks not suitable for horses or cattle, even, nor any animals before the Natives came to live on the land thousands of years ago from the Bering Strait, as theory goes.

"You are a free man of this city," says Allah in Sura Balad, *"and choose between Two Highways"*—of right conduct or wrong conduct in treating fellow human beings made equal in the sight of God, with regard to character and piety, for He shall judge between us all. Ameen.

And to have known that my ancestors were not treated as equals or that my ancestors may not have treated fellow humans as equals, I could not live too well with that.

But they were. as we were spoiled by a fair but messy system where twelve official creed heritages and five hundred linguistic communities strive together in one land, another place where many conquerors had come to stay.

Then there is the suffering here of an entire group of people whose children, grandchildren, and great-grandchildren are still haunted by that turmoil of mismanagement when they had been freed for a time in the land of the free, building the land to keep it free! To have built something from scratch and to have kept honor and trust as good citizenry yet still be subjected to trauma after trauma, not proving anything to people but their families' love or their love for God...

People say that group or that group is this way or that way. Why do they shout out things and curse the names of people they do not know? Why does that group throw stones instead of words? Why does that group have so many social problems now? Why is Africa tarnished now, and where have her riches gone?

When everything comes full circle, we thinkers see how each effect is related to each cause of man choosing right conduct or wrong conduct, affecting the larger global conduct. Even some rich Arabs in supposedly learned lands such as Saudi Arabia forget what the

Prophet of Equality taught them or the Predecessors of all Prophets taught them about treatment of people and how servants of God are mistreated, beaten and berated, some not treated as equals in Allah's sight. Surely, each man and each woman suffers inwardly for what each has done to the other where service matters before name, title, rank, or race. In God we trust, who created all for His purposes alone.

The War Is Not between Jesus and Muhammad (Peace Be on Them)

When people abandon you in times of
hardship, this is a sign that Allah wants
to take care of your struggles Himself.
—Imam Ash-Shafi-ee

Do not detest the misfortune that befall you, for
what you detest may be the cause of your salvation
and what you like may be the cause of your ruin.
[While I loved teaching more, writing may be
better for me than teaching in today's era.]
—Al-Hasan Al-Basree Rahimahullah

When the debate is lost, slander
becomes the tool of the losers.
—Socrates

Those who believe in the Quran, those who
follow the Jewish Scriptures, and the Sabians (the
ancients), and the Christians—Any who believe in
Allah and the Last Day, and work righteousness—
on them shall be no fear, nor shall they grieve.
—Holy Quran

June 10, 2020

The war is not between Jesus and Muhammad—neither one do I worship but love—

Or any other Faith-based path.

War seems to be between Darwinian Satanism and God, as it always was.

God always wins.

Let's just watch.

Yes, I would love to write about green fields again and butterflies' unchanged wings, lovely sunrises, and romantic walks in the desert during eventide.

But after so many pushes away from the mountainsides, I can only empathize with other beings' assault on their normal lives, never quite believing in the human desire for rescue missions, as blatant sinners seem to need so often.

I would love to write about the harmony between brothers and sisters of the universe or die like a hero while trying on a new masquerade that fits me to set the audience free.

But that is not me.

Nor ever will it be.

In seeking God, there has to be a struggle between what is good forever and what is not. And let them call me the evil one, their scary canary down the street of an old house of not seeming goodwill, until the eternal mercy and will of Allah ceases to live inside me.

Exhausting Work (As All Therapeutic Works Are)

*An education isn't how much you have
committed to memory, or even how much you
know. It's being able to differentiate between
what you know and what you don't.*
—Anatole France

May 7, 2021

Akka would say, when I was four,
"Keep on scribbling, my dear,"
Collecting and examining rocks in our Chicago backyard,
Where loving Shamim Chacha lived close to us, and Syed
Ghazanfar Imam mamu-jaan would warm my little hands
on the stove after school. The men of their time practiced
chivalry and warmth.
Akka's atmosphere, which he built with love, has kept my still
heart healing since youth. There, another redbird, just
like me,
Feeds off that lime-green blossoming tree.
One morsel of thought comes into me,
And there I go, healing and cleansed—receiving sustenance
Beyond understanding—more, much more than I deserve.
So in my sleep I write and dream, writing on napkins or my
phone in
My daily travels to confront reality of inside and the outside,
Understanding transitions between lifetimes.

It would have been nice not to have had trauma after
Trauma, unexpectedly delivering shocks to the brain of peace,
And it would have been fine to write about the two birds that
    come
Take their food from near my window, about the scent of bram-
    bles after rains...
But that's not what the will of God must have planned for me.
Maybe understanding is what I live for.

Literary Meeting

*For those who believe and work
righteousness, is every blessedness, and
a beautiful place of final return.*
—Sura "The Thunder"

*Truly I tell you, the one who believes in me will
also do the works that I do. [Jesus telling his people
to follow him instead of what throngs of people do.]*
—John 14:12

June 19, 2021

In the days of good Mr. George Hopper (as he always hired the conscientious, hardworking types since the school began), I had dared to join in some friendly critics' tea gathering for English teachers at a quaint country restaurant. Would I fit in? I didn't care then and still went. Of course, it was hot weather. Texas was wearing her bipolar weather everywhere.

I had felt flustered, discussing literature with people I wasn't so comfortable with. Maybe a more conservative Muslim would have gone straight home after work, but in those days, I believed in the system of professional social hours benefitting everyone.

While the tea went on, the critics enjoyed one another's voices; my thin porch chair creaked publicly. Embarrassed, I stood up quietly to find another chair and almost fell, papers and books falling, worrying for my baby inside.

Shy but still affected by critical points when needed, someone who was leaving the district for a more liberal one helped me up with genteel manners and no big to-do. With no gratitude expected, this was refreshing indeed. I could sense the young teacher's German upbringing—pious, suave, and used to fixing a situation rather than watching a mess from an angle wherever the silent majority sits.

Pregnancy never leaves most people feeling comfortable anyway, but how grateful I was for that simple kindness when most people were still taking notes, sipping tea, having dessert, and sharing more voices.

An environment can help us grow, or it can hinder our growth when compassion is or is not planted there.

In the good days of good Mr. Hopper, collaboration was a natural thing, needing no repair.

When Cancel Culture Turns Lethal, No One Knows.

In society, we do horrible things to one
another because we don't see the person it
affects. We don't see their face. We don't see
them as people. Which was the whole reason
the hood was built in the first place, to keep
the victims of apartheid out of sight and out
of mind. Because if white people ever saw
black [or colored people], as human, they
would see that slavery is unconscionable.
—Trevor Noah, *Born a Crime*
(a must-read memoir)

The proper response to conflict, whether it lies
within or without us, is disengagement.
—*I-Ching*

Catherine, at any rate, heard enough to feel, that
in suspecting General Tilney of either murdering
or shutting up his wife, she had scarcely sinned
against his character, or magnified his cruelty.
—Jane Austen, *Northanger Abbey*

May 6, 2021

No one knows if they'll become the next gothic, targeted person
    someday in a land
Where freedom isn't always here to stay,
Not for everyone anyway,
Where my educated parents came to live and work in good faith
    in God and country,
Accepted for their accomplishments, not out of pity's sake
Nor were they off on some metaphorical boat, for they sure
    were comfortable wherever they went,
Thinking they'd give their three precious daughters a stable
    learning
Atmosphere than Pakistan, where a lovely garden home was
    given to them
Just for teaching gifted students. Teaching is in our blood,
    apparently.
There is justice and the universal law of right and wrong. But
    freedom to pursue what you love has changed much since
    Mr. Trump came, going downhill ever since for uniquely
    educated persons of racial/creed difference
Yet how freedom showed her colors nicely in the eighties and
    nineties
While fixing social issues going on since the beginning—that
    dire slavery—
While the Final Prophet, as simple and unread as he was, had
    warned against slavery and treating women as property
    since 1,400 years ago
A blessing it was to free the slaves though rebel Muslims fake
Kept up with hierarchies as they still do today in parts of these
    states
How freedom shifts her vibrant colors here and there
And people keep jobs in high positions
Who don't even care for people except for when selling their
    wares
Freedom wears sometimes tartan, sometimes satin and lace,

Sometimes checkered, plaid, Scottish kilt, and India cotton
Surely, freedom keeps on changing her face from kindness to
Selfishness and in between humanoid ways.
In the nation, everyone comes to watch, a watchman's nation
Giving shelter in jobs in the land to whomever she deems perfect
Or less than perfect by the body type, stereotype, creed type,
Race type or being a castaway from Gilligan's Isle.
How? Why, even Germany, England, and Iraq, past Sadaam,
Past world brutality, have sought to treat each one the same:
      pursuit
Of happiness (for now) is just a virtual video game.
Why can't we do the same, if not better?
In Prophet's time, even women and colored people could raise
      a question, an objection or two—1,400 years ago. I stud-
      ied deeply when they ostracized whomever they thought
      I was or fight defense without transgressing if one needed
      to, but now we learn to become silent so that Supermen
Not so super anymore since COVID-19, could win an economic
      boost
In drug- and slave-trade racing, erasing womanhood
With some sad women's permission
Who'd rather trust Trump-Epstein men than God himself?

> God cannot change the condition of a
> people if man does not try to change himself.
> (Quranic wisdom)

The Given
Well of Our Self-Compassion
El Camino Real

Those who love to see scandal published,
broadcast among the Believers, will have a
grievous penalty in this life and the hereafter:
Allah knows (the truth), and you do not know.
—Sura 24, "The Light"

Therefore, this is what the Lord God says: I am
against your magic bands with which you ensnare
people like birds and I will tear them from your
arms. I will free the people you have ensnared
like birds. I will also tear off your veils (like
masks) and rescue my people from your hands, so
that they will no longer be prey in your hands.
Then you will know that I am the Lord. [Those
who claim to follow the Lord in their atrocities,
do they think they will not be answered?]
—Ezekiel 13:20–21

Maybe, just maybe, Allah keeps on giving me second chances to live again.

Wherever I was misjudged, accused of things I was never guilty of and wherever I was no terrorist, instigator, snake, narcissist, or shelled creature except when covering my ears from excessive noise or drones hovering about wherever I happened to be, once we understand that many before us were treated in similar ways (maybe not as harshly for as long), then we come to see that instigators need to seek some help before their rage holds them in control of everything else.

Maybe just for being so darned conscientious all the time, Allah rewards us in diverse ways, and I can live in divergent ways to let my blessed parents know that still I tried surviving and never gave up from succeeding in the way of God who has given me everything in spite of myself.

Conroe,
Del Lago Being in One's Element
A School Academic Retreat under
Ms. Sue Pope's Fair Supervision

*Don't you see that it is Allah whose praise all
things in the heavens and on earth do celebrate,
and the birds of the air with wings outspread?
Each one knows its own mode of prayer and
praise. And Allah knows well all that they do...
Don't you see that Allah makes the clouds move
gently, then joins them together, then makes
them into a heap? Then you will see rain issue
forth from their midst. And He sends down
from the sky mountain masses of clouds... He
strikes wherewith whom He pleases and He
turns it away from whom He please. [Amen.]*
—Sura 24, "The Light"

June 2014

Each teacher was given just enough space to enjoy nature and
people/colleagues in his/her own special ways. We could take our
notebooks out and record ideas. We could discuss the topics in mul-
tifarious groups without acting as if we were grouping into "likes"
and "dislikes."

While Ms. Sue Pope and I had different views about teaching, leadership, or student-behavior treatment, there was a sense of deep, professional respect for our individual identities. It was also a different era in teaching. People did not have to choose some "perfect red" or "perfect blue." We did not have to sacrifice our careers for the politics of the day.

I even questioned Ms. Pope on certain ideas, and she would listen to me even if she disagreed. This was what I thought America was all about: freedom for people to agree to disagree. She had not known much about my religious proclivities and traditions, and I had known a few basic things about hers without having studied the diverse Bibles as I did after my experiences with the Trump-inspired administration that sandwiched every school problem with Trump's own thinking. Ms. Pope's leadership style was neutral, and neutrality keeps people believing in one's leadership even if neutrality shifts somewhat in one's own studied position.

This next poem is one of my favorites in this collection as I was free to be myself, free to be a good teacher without feeling shame for being unique, and free to engage properly and professionally with all teachers during lunch or breakfast (delicious breakfast, by the way) without being bullied into saying fake things I did not believe. I still knew that I would not be able to strive for anything higher than teaching even if I were qualified, and that did disappoint me. However, my teaching was not questioned when Ms. Pope was around. This made me respect her leadership personality.

With Mr. George Hopper and Dr. Michael Worthy, I was treated respectfully as a full person with all my rights and privileges, free to soar as an "eagle" or "goose," spreading my wings as high as I chose to instruct my students in all the ways I knew. When power comes into safe, sturdy hands, people will blossom. When power comes into self-centered hands, pretending to do good things for all staff but only doing well for the few, any staff crumbles. And education suffers while students become objects, minions, and one-sided persons with depressed goals. When a "leader" or a "society" singles us out, we tend to become defensive, afraid, depressed, and anxious—all ingredients of a failed leadership. Failed leadership cannot just fly off to

Florida and improve the comers of the land by ego alone or by using God's name alone.

Humane work needs to be done with egalitarian treatment for any land or organization so that all people, not a small few, have the ability to be in their complete element—to be true to themselves while working hard on job projects or team planning to reach larger company goals. If some people are conveniently left out from the company's dreams and goals, then not everyone is being true to their precepts of fine treatment, and inevitably, people begin to short-change themselves from what or who they could become. A pithy wisdom in Sura Bee reminds one of this concept of treating people with the same treatment we want for ourselves and our own loved ones:

> And do not take your oaths, to practice deception between yourselves, with the result that someone's foot may slip up after it was firmly planted, and you may have to taste the evil con-sequences of having hindered men and women from the Path of God, as mighty Wrath descends on you.

Sure, this is a strong warning from the Wise One for us regular human beings, yet when we think deeply of what can happen to people if we play tricks on them, those tricks may fall back on us, causing us inner damage and a lack of inner peace. Sometimes, one's own family members play tricks on us; other times, it is people we have loved all of our lives from childhood or colleges. Regardless, it takes much effort to be in one's own element as lovely birds of the sky that are always in harmony no matter what chaos is surrounding their sceneries and travel flights.

This takes more than effort and perseverance. It requires con-sistency, understanding, and a tearing down of bad walls instead of building expensive walls at the cost of degrading/breaking up fam-ilies. It requires passion with tenacity, sincerity without excessive masks on top of masks, and fairness for unison to happen in a chaotic environment swayed by unnecessary pressures.

Good leaders and good teachers ask, "How would I feel if such and such were to happen to me? Do I feel content in front of God Almighty (or at least my conscience) that I have treated people the ways I want to be treated?" Selfish leaders want popularity and wealth at the cost of brutalizing their most loyal staff members. Might makes right to them. Too bad they hadn't read the works of the evolutionary scientist who did not make racial superiority claims six hundred years before Darwin: Al-Tusi from the Mediterranean. Too bad mighty leaders with complex superiority/inferiority issues did not study the patterns of birds traveling together in harmony. Everything is possible; nature teaches us this through God's help. Only He knows why He created whom and where, why, and in what capacity. We only think we know. The more we think we know the less we know, as the aphorism goes.

What does watching nature in harmony and chaos require? The mind's alignment with the heart, the heart's alignment with the soul, and the soul's alignment with the brain. Nature watched closely is a lifelong lesson. Human nature watched for highlighted error (in judgment) is a lesson that needs to be reviewed and revisited, for the humanoid and we humans may be more in transition than nature herself. While being in one's element may not seem substantial in today's dog-eat-dog, competitive world, being in one's element is my aspiration and has always been since childhood years.

There was an entire essay-letter that once my dad sent me in college, and another time, my mom sent me one after marriage. These treated the theme of being in one's element no matter what chaos or harmony may be happening outside of us. I suppose the blessed parents were the first healers after God.

The smallest things would surprise me, excite me, enrich my sensibilities further, or delight me for no obvious reasons whatsoever. This experience of being fascinated with everything—the happy and the sad, the light and the dark, the ebullient and the gloomy, the glittering and the opaque aspects of reality—took me to other layers of thought as in rainbows of sight, sound, intuition, etc. A thoughtful young person in my fifth period who I was blessed to teach decades ago noted that many people have to see things that they understand or feel things that are relatable to reach other levels of intuition and newer levels of cognition.

This interesting perception was in sync with my own ideal realities of seeking answers to life's bigger questions beyond what the eye beholds on a daily basis. There is nothing mystical about perception and intuition; rather, we each find our paths to knowledge and intuition based on our childhood experiences. If we capture the child within ourselves since the early years and understand why we became the way we grew up, then we can problem-solve our later experiences, content in the acceptance that what is meant to happen will happen no matter how we try to be part and parcel of any unknown environment.

To be wrangling with the self's various facets and forces is to be in tune with finding our own possibilities that God has given us, and these potentialities may not necessarily be what other fellow humans see as successful or growth-oriented. But that is irrelevant. We each find uniquely suited aspects of reality that help us along our personal paths toward life discovery beyond ourselves, beyond the forces of our own egos, and beyond what we think we know until some level of satisfaction and peace are achieved.

Peace, for me, is the greatest achievement. I know for many, it is money, love, fame, excitement, collections of things and people, status, worldly honor, etc. But peace truly is an achievement when stressors are heightened as a flashlight points in one's direction. And this has come from not attaching myself too much to anyone or anything, just enough, while relying on the Almighty for my nurturance. Every day, I look at how the birds fly seemingly needing assistance from their peers, and some go to their destinations in congregations; others fly alone to wherever they consider their temporal homes. No bird that I have ever seen seems to be concerned with how many feathers they have been given or how their feathers glitter compared to other feathers. They are living in their elements, seeking solace from their Maker or what seems like nature's shelter to many people. That nature can also be destructive, yet the birds do not seem to mind. This is their lifestyle: to live in simple ways. God tells in *The Narration* of an aspect of what many Sufis call the essence of the Quran: "The material things which you are given are but the conveniences of this life and the glitter thereof; but that which is with Allah is better and more enduring: will you not then be wise?"

It is a choice for me to follow the glittering path of materialism, making myself an allurement to myself and others, or to follow a simple path that sees conveniences as just that but nothing more. Conveniences do not have to be trappings but are what they are: convenient mechanisms to try and simply live. Yet paradoxically, the more man/woman invents wondrous conveniences with which to simply live, the more people get engrossed in the complexities of those conveniences until boredom and tomfoolery (to use an archaic term) set in one's life, making it so complex that people get confused about who they want to be and where they think they are going. What we have and own, with whom we associate, or with which rich companies we spend our time do not define our essence as people. We are who we wish to be no matter what our religion, race, inner creed, social strata, hierarchy, etc. We exist. And how grateful I am for existence—my own and everybody else's.

Even those who choose to live their lives engulfed in deception or glamorous crimes have a right to live. Who are we to take or steal their lives away? For criminals, too, are guiding people in how not to live if one's goal is inner peace. If one's goal is life's conveniences and material pleasures all the time, such people may find temporary ways toward peace, but certain habits and associations can come back to steal their peace. And while the convenient life of not being in touch with one's element and knowing our strengths and weaknesses may not seem important on one's separate path to somewhere or something, the life of conveniences can surely bring us down from our aspirations so that we become restless, insecure, uncomfortable with our essence, and always on the lookout for who truly sees us for what we are. This could not be a comfortable reality.

Conroe, Del Lago

written while attending an excellent academic
retreat led by Principal Sue Pope

*The value of life lies not in the length of
days, but in the use we make of them...
whether you find satisfaction in life depends
not on your tale of years, but on your will.*
　　　　　　　—Michel de Montaigne

And to your Lord turn all your attention.
　　　　　　　—Sura 95

June 2014

　　All in a line the geese go,
　　Migrants in the sky;
　　Something whistles, something stirs
　　Across time.

　　Ducks squabble in their element,
　　Pine rustles into pine;
　　Every dormant creature
　　Rises graciously.

　　Let the skeptic and the faithful
　　Rejoice along the way.
　　This dance of geese may come and go—
　　Wildlife pantomime.

Let foes of peace curse wakes of wonder
As dusk pours into day;
Everywhere in nature's dance,
New life stirs with grace.

Men of war raze any populace;
Some shield their eyes and hearts.
Still, across tides of infants' blood,
Each tells its side of carnage.

In rage storms or in war zones,
Men are bent on killing divergent men.
In fear, we claim ambivalence
To justify our clawing.

Look onward: in line the geese go
Without cease-fire or campaigns;
Something tells them how to fly
Across time in unison!

Imagine All the Youngest Children

Let tenderness pour from your eyes the way the
sun gazes warmly on the earth…let's toast every
rung we've climbed on evolution's ladder.
—Hafiz

May 24, 2021

Imagine all the youngest children who must deal with the consequences of elders' bad choices, careless words, tirades, their laziness or super-ambitions gone awry or their lack of being in tune with themselves on any given day, treating their loved ones as verbal punching bags for their own lost days.

Some great people place their children in trusted hands where each second is a damage to the child's brain; others select even their day care teachers with the perfect scrutiny as if each family's breath depended on it.

Mango Drink Misplaced and Found

*More inheritance? Love creates a synchronicity
with what love loves…bring yourself, again,
into the presence of God, someone who
knows God, for more inheritance is there
for you. Hold hands with the Buddha, if a
living saint's warmth has been forgotten.*

—Hafiz

May 19, 2021

Misplacing the mango drink, I looked in all four rooms, even the hallway with unopened packages—not there, the drink.

So Khursheed, my darling, went to look in four different spots for my drink in the middle of his work time that day.

Still not there.

Like many misplaced things and misplaced people, misplaced nations with misplaced hopes and dreams, and misplaced plans for existence everything was where it should be.

The mango drink was in front of the vase in front of my face.

People are always looking for the right way to do something— their ways often getting found or misplaced by design, it seems, to be retaught and reconnected for when they are ready and willing to see.

I thought I, too, was a misplaced person in the wrong country, the wrong era, as it often seems to those who stick out somewhere.

But I am where I should be through one who plans whatever should be.

Until we humans ourselves misplace ourselves and our mango drinks.

So we find that elixir that fits our nature without getting drunk on the elixir's nature so that we may still sense our purpose there.

It's not the job that fits people; people make themselves fit the job/home to suit their elixir: the job's purposes.

Education—is it suffering because people choose it as an option or a prime passion—a job satisfaction? Learning—is it satisfactory, or is it only a job out of boredom?

Some think they are too smart for education, too smart for an institution, not finding that elixir that stems from within.

Not fitting in might be even better, then, rather than flexing each tense muscle to meet some uppity person's personal goals or flexing oneself into finding that joy again where joy is none, only to find selfishness at the cost of everyone's learning effervescence.

At the DPS
Microcosm of a Public School with
Potential and Tact

> *More attentive than any lover or parent is*
> *really God to us, but our gauge of judgement is*
> *impaired by the world's values, and our bodies*
> *often dominant over our spirit realm. / A young*
> *child first learning to walk and very likely to*
> *fall may be allowed to do so by a wise guardian*
> *or teacher / if there is a soft mat beneath its*
> *body that will cushion it from harm / There*
> *is a soft mg you can place around others it is*
> *forgiveness, it is charity. / We are still learning*
> *to walk—and fly—in ways; kin help each*
> *other. And everything that I am related to.*
> —Hafiz, "Falling on a Soft Mat"

May 24, 2021

In general, people everywhere, but especially here at the DPS,
Have incredible manners.
When the purpose is clear, manners are there.
How could schools use this knowledge of the ordinary places
    that bring on extraordinary outcomes?
When thunder strikes, a certain calmness resides in people, nor-
    mally chaotic,
Keeping harm away from themselves and everyone near them.

When lightning happens sooner than expected,
The calmest minds needn't rely on drugs or alcoholic rises.
In public places, where rules are clear and subtly enforced
By subtle people who know how to direct the crowd,
People behave—no shouting needed nor even a rod, nor Tasers
    nor guns.
Corona, too, has been an enforcer in places not used to subtle
    enforcers.
COVID-19 has taught what God had given, but people could
    not listen before: close ones who thought doors were clos-
    ing just for them.
That God is there and everywhere people choose to behave in
    orderly procession amid chaos outside, no man needed
    there—no man with sticks, no woman following sticks.
    Subtle enforcers that teach through miseries that
Whatever happens anywhere shall come anyway, no excitement
    needed amid that crowd.
Not so distant is that Lord of all the universes, making all suf-
    fering—visible and invisible—ease away after hardship
    or timely death if we care to know the orders existing
    beyond our small selves.
At the DPS, meanwhile, everybody has a plan.
Who cares here if our grammar is lacking?
For manners shall help restore this landscape of violence on
    streets
Much, much more than pretty grammar or extra knowledge
    from anywhere.
At the DPS in Spring, Texas, and the one in San Antonio, I
    meet the kind of people who could have been teachers,
    gracefully handling hundreds and hundreds of clients at
    a time with no rage,
Patient in adversity,
Tolerant of small faults,
Forgiving of one's impulses in reaching high goals fast.

Meeting people where they are at: what youngsters need to see
    in older people who still have grace and tact placed in
    them by God's mercy
Instead of wrath.

One's Weight in Gold or How We See Ourselves

Those who believe in the Quran, and those who follow the Jewish scriptures, and the Christians and the Sabians, (the ancients), and who believe in Allah and the Last Day, and work righteousness, shall have their reward with their Lord: on them shall be no fear, nor shall they grieve. [We are called to be just and fair to all humanity's sisters and brothers since we are said to be of Prophet Adam and Hawaa's progeny since the birth of human beings; this is why I still have hope for a democracy that is dying slowly as classes struggle to be better than each other when God has asked us to treat each member equally even though we disagree on smaller, finer points in each group's struggle in a race-based society that may seem displeasing to the Lord, who made one and all.] And remember, We took your Covenant and We raised above you the towering height of Mount Sinai: saying, "Hold firmly to what We have given you and bring ever remembrance what is therein: perchance you may fear Allah. But you turned back thereafter: had it not been for the Grace and Mercy of Allah to you, you had surely had been among the lost."

—Sura 2; emphasis added

May 24, 2021

Better to be poor enough and taken care of nicely and willfully
Than work beside self-chosen careless whisperers with sneaky
    side offices,
Stuck inside hierarchies of class hierarchies, only to be mocked
    by those under them or over them for being good enough
Or not so good enough by earthlings' standards.
Better to be taken for the "sand *izwer*" (a group called me) than
    a high-ranking teacher of internal majesty
Better to be called a cat to be skinned than try fitting into a
    skinny whore's closet I wouldn't want to be seen in or near
Better to be tougher on myself and fight the evil left over in
    me than kill misogynists' mockingbirds or join Zionists
    burning buildings
Better to be an honest immigrants' daughter of married love
    than be a bastardized child of superiority
For Prophet Ismail is misjudged for being born of blessed
    Hagira's tribe by Allah's permission
Than pretend myself a "chosen people," wiping off their cousins
    from the face of the earth
Better to be a hybrid American of Indo-Semitic and Indo-
    Subcontinental descent, a cosmopolite of different
    conscience,
Than be some elite queen lady who won't be accepted by English
    royalty,
Descending supposedly by one cousin far, far away from Fatima
    Honorable of nobility.
Better to be a drenched sparrow in the rain than a peacock shin-
    ing all its feathers at once
In the sun for anyone to see.
No, not every woman wants to be queen of any domain
Some of us are content being servants of God in any given
    domain
Amen

To Be a Mom

*Inside, the strength of simplicity and
self-knowledge; outside, the beauty
of acceptance and gentleness.*
        —I Ching

*In the Law of Equality there is saving of Life
to you, O you men of understanding; that
you may restrain yourselves… For Allah is to
all people most surely full of kindness, Most
Merciful. [His kindness is akin to a billion
kindnesses of all mothers who would only do
good, conscious good as much as possible, for their
children—His kindness is so great that we forget
who makes us kind sometimes when we have
witnessed earthlings' angry people. Ameen.]*
        —Sura 2

*No one needs to be a tiger to solve
life's problems, or to find joy.*
        —Cousin Tanveer

May 24, 2021

To be a mom may not seem glamorous nor even rewarding all the time on outward appearances.

It may not be for everyone in a realm when success is often determined by aggressiveness and how much we can win to keep to ourselves anew for ages.

When Grandfather Syed Jafar Imam, in Bihar, near Gaya (near where Gautama Buddha once reached Nirvana), stood in white kurta-pajama, hands tied behind his back, and Grandmother Abunnisa sat wearing her crisp white cotton sari, covered from head to foot with almond eyes showing, we children sat on the porch swing, moving like a pendulum.

I still remember, though I was less than four, visiting from Chicago via Pakistan and back to India where Ammi was born.

Some funny person asked us children, "What will you become someday?"

"A doctor," said a cousin. "A lawyer like you," said another to Grandfather, Nana Aba.

Someone said, "Engineer," and other good professions. I couldn't think of anything, so I looked at my mom, radiant and blossoming in her floral sari waving in the wind.

"*Main ammi banungi, ammi banungi.*" A mom is what I wanted to be.

And everybody laughed, I still remember. My braids slid back toward my face, which was turning hot from embarrassment. Ammi smiled. The laughter stopped. All the cousins on the porch swing were loved, hugged tightly.

Who knew that my accidental words would be my truest calling even before teaching, though it may not show as I am not the traditional mom (from anywhere), watching each child growing as separate nations grow: within their own elements, blossoming.

On Your Birthday

And when you judge between man and man:
that you judge with justice: verily how excellent
is the teaching which He gives you. For Allah
is He who hears and sees all things. [Amen.]
    —Sura 4, "The Women/Nisa"

The presence of a Perfect One reaches a seed
that is planted in you. [InshaAllah.]
    —Hafiz

May 23, 2021

The day you were born
Was the day I knew—
Something had to be right with the world.
Each child has inborn traits
That Divine Mercy gave in flux.
Abundance—to live with kindness or otherwise,
Practical sense—to be that person one can trust,
Making this realm a better place
Not for money, envy, greed, or lust
But for the sake of the Highest Consciousness—whom many
  trust
In times of sorrow, in times of peace,
Who makes things right no matter how wronged,
For in self-pity, no one lives strong.
Giving, receiving, accepting, and glorifying Beloved's name
In justice, peace, mercy, or wisdom,

In any field you choose to do.
In flux is the world, in flux are we.
Nothing ever stays the same,
Ready and *razi* for practiced change,
Hoping with faith, practiced truths,
Timeless for each one as they are.
Why ever force anyone to be other
Than how they are, leading to growth
In acceptance of how Divine made each
For whichever purpose placed on earth?
How small are we indeed. How small.
How large the globe where life-forms abide
In lovely, practiced diversity.
When you were born, Akka said you'd speak,
And each would listen; your words would matter,
Paralleling thoughts we'd like to say.
How blessed am I that you're my child
And each of you, my friend, as I still grow
—trusting you to say your peace—
And live with practiced sensibilities
No matter how tough life seems to be.
Ameen.

Old Souls and Youth
Twelve Pink Roses Bloom and Fade

One day Allah will gather the Messengers (of all tribes) together, and ask: 'What was the response you received from men to your teaching?" They will say: 'We have no knowledge: it is You who knows in full all that is hidden. [Ameen.]
—Sura 5

So, Moses cried out to the Lord, and the Lord showed him a tree. When he threw it into the water, the water became drinkable. The Lord made a statute and ordinance for them at Marah, and he tested them there. He said, "If you will carefully obey the Lord your God, do what is right in His sight, pay attention to His commands, and keep all His statutes, I will not inflict any illnesses on you that I inflicted on the Egyptians. For I am the Lord who heals you. Then came to Elim, where there were twelve springs and seventy date palms, and they camped there by the water." [Amen.]
—Exodus 15:25–27

June 8

Twelve pink roses fading now,
As each tribe lost its root from where humanity's languages were
    written
Early on—lost purpose and directions
On human faces, filthy boots
What would happen if we, human tribes of flowers budding
    into grace,
Would try listening anyway
Despite our whims and excess desires for life's glittering things?
Why would Lord God hear a call if men invest in lies,
fighting Him instead of bowing down to Him? To the left, the
    copper tree frowns,
Hanging its fruits below, borrowing each from every root the
Same needs that humans share in shelter or renown.
Who says some are less or worse
The names I've heard them call?
Unless they live in the devil's care,
Not caressed by Good above,
Stuck in deep despair of piling-up worldly goods
While ostracizing people or bombing ones who
Built their own lands' space.
Do they think God can't listen?
Cain and Abel fought hard and cold;
Youth forgets who began,
For conflict reduction is as vast as
The Red Sea parting over again.
Destiny we humans think we make,
Planning scheme upon each scheme
As human vampires fabricate
The Planner's greater scheme
So each one tries to please its kind,
Roses trampling on each other's thorns,
Inching away from nature's ways
Then screaming for each one being born.

The money tree, it stands upright,
Branching in all directions;
No leaves trespass on others' breaths
Or pathologies, breathing in collaboration.
But humans, how spoiled and soiled we are—
Uncouth, uncomfortable with Higher Unity,
Cain killing Abel for no reason but the impulse
Of the moment.
We push and push people's nuclear buttons
Instead of finding solace or beauty in a moment,
pointing the finger where the trigger is:
Twelve roses spring upward to bloom
From Almighty's own gracious ways,
Some made to wither sooner than the weather
As thorns dig inside the pulse of them.
Few tribes from the twelve get a chance on earth,
And so we Semitic gravitate
Back to God from where we are. Amen

June 8
Critics They Call Vampires Who Know Not What Vampires Are

It is Allah who begins the process of Creation; then,
repeats it; then you shall be brought back to Him.
        —Sura "The Roman Empire" (a Quranic
                prophecy of how the Romans won)

Do not join the wicked to be a malicious witness.
You must not follow a crowd in wrongdoing.
Do not testily in a lawsuit and go along with a
crowd to pervert justice. Do not show favoritism
to a poor person in his lawsuit… You must not
deny justice to a poor person among you in his
lawsuit. Stay far away from a false accusation.
Do not kill the innocent and the just, because I
will not justify the guilty. You must not take a
bribe, for a bribe blinds the clear-sighted and
corrupts the words of the righteous. You must
not oppress a resident alien; you yourselves know
how it feels to be a resident alien because you
were resident aliens in the land of Egypt.
                        —Exodus 23:1–2, 6–9

> *The Hill-Brow police station looks exactly*
> *like every other police station in South Africa.*
> *They were all built by the same contractor at*
> *the height of apartheid—separate nodes in the*
> *central nervous system of a police state. If you*
> *were blindfolded and taken from one to the other,*
> *you probably wouldn't even know that you'd*
> *changed locations. They're sterile, institutional,*
> *with fluorescent lights and cheap floor tile, like*
> *a hospital. [Every educated person should read*
> *Trevor Noah's memoir for life-long learning.]*
> —Trevor Noah, *Born a Crime*

June 8

We critics are termed vampires, who know not what vampires
    really are,
Lovers of all?
Not even themselves, most tragic of all.
For critics aren't supposed to offer sense in the nonsensical
    "realist"
Traumas that most everyone will face sooner or later
Even when decent, good intentions
Have been made to seem poisonous,
Defending one's own self or others'
Trodden bodies.
True vampires come out of any brambly bush
They don't do family life, nor can they stand being alone
Rather, they live from fire to fire,
Burning most books as Montag, out of spite.
Never stopping to wonder how we got from over there
To here or transcended primates' competitive fears,
Vampires are good at creating unnecessary angst
When people could be calm in their own balms.
Maybe there may come a time
When security will not matter, not for families,

Companies, or individuals, as each will live again
In retaliation's stone age, immune to blood and war
Barely existing under shadows of vampires'
Vanguards and artillery weapons
Using feel-good emojis
They haven't felt or known. (Astaghfimllah/God Forbid).

Curiosity is the
Learners' Way (Alistair Reid)
Dystopia's Utopia

Do they not look at the Camels, how they are
made? And at the sky, how it is raised? [Curiosity
for learning anything is part and parcel of
Islam and Quran, thus leading to scientific and
literary inquiries/discoveries.] Surely we did
not give birth to ourselves! Alhumdullilah.

—Sura 88

Breakthroughs happen when we are
not drawn back into bad habits.

—*I Ching*

June 7

When a young journalist and her medicine buddy
Asked a certain fancy lady, "Why? Please tell us, why,"
The fancy pocket read the questioning letter and said
With Kleenex on face for the first time in ages,
"I really didn't have a reason to do it to her that way
That many times. No,
I had no reason."
And suddenly she appeared as small as a watch
From *Clockwork Orange* in imperfect shape
(It was understood by many solid ones

90

That the real perpetrators got away and should have been
    punished
Or humiliated for those unmentionable acts I shall not name
    again).
"Then why?" asked the young intellectuals. "Why?
And how could you, after such a long set of loyal years,
Working with your own children, and a few punishments
So harsh, have no due process for no obvious reasons?"
Petrified as stone, the strongly connected watch piece stood
In silent scrutiny before wiser youth. "How could you?"
Receiving rare visitors only
But not for "smaller" occasions.
No one knows how, why, or by what mean
Assumptions and projections of smear campaigners
One's life career takes the wrong turn. No one knows
When it could be them by inward narcissism
Expressed in depression's delirium
When they, too, had prepared decades and decades of
Career reformation without protesters' revolutions
In bloody ways, dividing and conquering Mary and Elizabeth
To appease old King Henry's lust-feuding ways in the death
    towers'
Unheedful systems,
Where freedom's rings bragged on and on
Under mighty badge surveillance
As if Higher Law wasn't watching them
Go down the Tower of London.

Honorary House Visited in England

Truly, man was created very impatient;
fretful when evil touches him; and
miserly when good reaches him. Not so
those devoted to Prayer. [Ameen.]
—Sura 70

Better a little with righteousness, than
great income with injustice. [Amen.]
—Proverbs 16:8

At some point one's prayers will become
so powerful that they can shake a full tree
in an orchard in heaven and fruit will
roll through the streets in this world.
—Hafiz

June 7

On the surface, the hostess's house didn't have as much as they
did here.
But the house was a home as it was Generosity's guest first.
As I sit eating my mozzarellas, weeping at society's changes and
sipping
From Sonic's iced limeade, the house in front reminds me
Of a garden house in England with small balcony and
A green yard of a million flowers from everywhere
Where British embraced Indian foods and cultures
Long ago, even more then Indians. I like British food more.

The homey people even offered up their small dinette for us
As if we were permanently on vacation—fancy talk never for
    them,
Gentle ways, never stuck up.
They, too, had ups and downs, wasting gas
For huffs and puffs. They, too, had Anglican Christians or
    humanist
Traditions, Hindus, Muslims, or agnostics. It didn't matter
In that trip or the next one or the next one
Where each regular sentient carried Wordsworth's sonnets in
    their hearts—
How green is England still—innate wisdom in their global,
    accommodating minds.
What do schools teach our youngsters now? To hurt in history's
    pain
Or to heal by humankind's global gains?
Or to involve students in sticky territorial wars,
Dividing people into classes, hierarchical, till everyone falls
    somewhere beyond the earth?
When it's anyone's turn to be harassed by some elitist mob,
Sunglasses won't come in handy to reverse time's aching clocks.
(Still, I do forgive. Yet as President Biden says,
I/we must remember to keep mental learning alive and active
And not become the actions
We Democrats and equality-thinking Republicans do despise.)

Wasn't Rough Man Created So Impatient?

Truly, man was created very impatient; fretful when evil touches him; and miserly when good reaches him. No so those devoted to Prayer.
—Sura 70

All who make idols are nothing and what they treasure benefits no one. Their witnesses do not see or know anything, so they will be put to shame.
—Isaiah 44:9

It is certainly not good to fine an innocent person or to beat a noble for his honesty.
—Proverbs 17:26

Righteousness exalts a nation, but sin is a disgrace to any people.
—Proverbs 14:34

Don't those who plan evil go astray? But those who plan good find loyalty and faithfulness.
—Proverbs 14:22

O my father! Do not serve Satan: for Satan is a rebel against Allah Most Gracious.
—Sura Maryam 19

Thus evil indeed is the abode of the arrogant.
[Quran does not speak of naked Houris
disorienting man in Paradise for doing
martyrdom on earth, as false orators like to say.]
—Sura 16:29

June 7

Maybe it was good that mean people kept interrupting well-planned secular lessons where students did most of the talking about books and where they shared portfolio discussions with me as a facilitator instead of a know-it-all.

Maybe it was good that their leaders microaggressively spied on me in large mobs at a time, sending their latest student teachers so that they'd rid themselves of that one pesky, observant Muslim and find others like her in their styles, smiling all the same—those fake, gritty smiles—between aggressive impulses.

Maybe Allah is using me for His own purposes as His law-abiding servant who shall not stoop to popular fad crimes or cheapness for the masses, lusting to get ahead in this life.

It is actually pleasing to please Him in times of my suffering in educational enterprises where a broader education doesn't matter much anymore.

"Do y'all kill people in Ramadan?" asked a young teacher impetuously during team, as if post-9-11 didn't teach her anything.

"Is she teaching Shariah Law?" asked the raging, new director from junior high, walking in without a plan. (Later I find out that Shariah Law offers justice for children as parents are expected to be benign caretakers.)

"*Is she crazy?*" the Trumpians would ask their own kinds in the hallways each time I was elected to supervise their student prom or speak names at graduation.

And all the additional stupid questions that teachers should have known as basic, gifted educators.

Hatred has a funny way of laughing at anything that is not ludicrous.

I guess now I have found the greatest treasure of all: reading the Quran for pleasure (even more than Shakespeare), seeking His eternal mercy just for being me, not pleasing anybody for the sake of a job. Instead of memorizing Shakespeare plays for fun, I now try to learn verses from the Quran, giving me more comfort from a world that is unholy.

I wondered as they shamelessly dragged me down their hallway for no crime that I committed, without due process, grabbing my arms and private areas, humiliating me, how they can brainwash students with their canned lesson plans, but I couldn't not let students ask literary questions or teach them about literature. They could teach worksheets, but I could no longer help students find their careers or help save them from suicides from pressures they were drowning in.

As a practical young family said, influenced then by friends, of course, "You have a wide knowledge of unnecessary things for no reason," and even that is okay now.

Allah must have had this plan for me to turn to Him all along and to let me suffer just enough but not too much, surviving in the worldly ways that never appealed to me anyway.

Why do so many humans invest their time and energies in believing in humans who end up doing crimes and living double lives?

Why do we join any field that doesn't even align its curriculum to universal values so that people could get along better in their own families, let alone the larger society anywhere, where sooner or later, they, too, may not belong and where belongingness means servanthood to people instead of Almighty God?

Does every man long to enter the Garden of
Bliss? By no means! (Sura "The Ways of Ascent")

On Welcoming President Obama

*Because Allah will never change the Grace
which He has bestowed on a people until they
change what is in their own souls: and verily
Allah is He who hears and knows all things.*
—Sura 8

*L et there arise out of you a band of people inviting
to all that is good, enjoining what is right, and
forbidding what is wrong: they are the ones who
attain felicity… Not all are alike: of the People
of the Book are a portion that stand for the right;
they rehearse the Signs of God all night long,
and they prostrate themselves in adoration.*
—Sura 3

Tumult and oppression are worse than slaughter.
—Sura 2

*Let the people of the Gospel judge by what Allah
has revealed therein. If any fail to judge by the
light of what Allah has revealed, they are no
better than those who rebel. If Allah had so
willed, He would have made you a single people,
but His Plan is to test you in what He has
given you: so strive as in a race in all virtues.*
—Sura 5

*If anyone digs a pit, they themselves will fall into
it: If anyone rolls a stone, it will roll back on them.*
—Proverbs 26:27

*I do call to witness this City; you are a free man
of this City... Does man think that none beholds
him? Have we not made for man a pair of eyes?
And a tongue, and a pair of lips? And shown
him the two highways [of correct and incorrect
behaviors through free will]... And what will
explain to you the path that is steep? It is in freeing
the bondman, or the giving of food in a day of
privation...or to the indigent down in the dust.*
—Sura 90

Shock of All Shocks

*And among His Signs is the creation of the
heavens and the earth, and the variations
in your languages and your colors: verily in
that are the Signs for those who know.*
　　　　　　—Sura "The Roman Empire"

June 7

When one institution first learned about President Obama
being elected, I felt as if I hadn't lived long enough in the nation to
notice how polarized in hatred it already was.

That was the first sign to me as an ingenue who had trusted
too many in good faith that American racism was more common
than cherry and apple pies and was disguised as much as a footballer
severely injured, standing up as if he were all right.

Race problems? Now commercials are playing as if there were no
race problems.

Creed problems? Forget creed problems; that's too global for the
average person.

On the intercom are the institution holder's words, which I
shall try to paraphrase:

> Okay, y'all just sit tightly now. *As if every-
> one was on a hazardous airplane ride and about to
> come crashing soon because a Black man had taken
> office by the people's vote.]* I realize that things are
> really changing. Let's not get overworked [as if
> a pandemic were already about to start—maybe

God answered that]. Just go to y'all's classes. Act
normal. See? Things could get worse.

The Black students from my gifted classes were made to feel like
winning foreigners on their own soil!

It was as if their mamas, grandpas, and papas had done nothing
to build this nation after all!

Some wore bright-colored orange-and-black Obama T-shirts
with American flags while (many) quietly racist English teachers had
placed small Confederate flags in the hollow corners of their ironed
shirts as if supporting a private Kool conference group based on their
race alone!

It was mind-boggling that only a few of my conscientious White
students were in the room or coming to school, for the administrators made it clear how they were supposed to feel.

It was mind-boggling to one who grew up in a natural diversity of Christians and Catholics who practiced their Christianity,
good Jews, Hindus, Muslims, Sikhs, Agnostics, gays, and undeclared
in the New Jersey, New York, and Chicago neighborhoods, where
everybody used to belong.

Why, why, why would a preacher lady and her minions, her
muscular handymen, feel so threatened? *I didn't understand. So
scared?* So tightwad about her generosity, buried somewhere between
love of Christ and sainthood?

Then I knew why, at every chance, the upward-bound leader
would find ways to do small and large wrongs to me: I was the double
whammy for her...a darkie fat person ostracized for being unusual in
style and presentation.

And I dared to remain a Muslim in spite of all that.

Those Who Cannot Even Honor
the Tortured Man after Death

Then, contemplate, O man! The memorials
of Allah's mercy! How He gives life to the
earth after its death: verily the same will
give life to the men who are dead: for He
has power over all things. [Amen.]
—Sura 30

Discipline is harsh for the one who leaves the
path; the one who hates correction will die. [Here,
death seems to mean both deaths—life from earth,
and future possible life due to transgressions.]
—Proverbs 15:10

June 9

I find it ironic that (some of) those who say they believe in law and order find selective law and order to give.

When George Floyd was murdered by torture (nobody had declared him the world's only hero but someone distinct whose death was not in vain)—no, he should not have received torture at the hands of the law, which is there to protect any man or woman in this land, not make a mockery of one who came equally in the name of the Lord.

But he wasn't popular by the local "friends" of certain clubs who betrayed him. Would you want to be killed by any bigots or former friends on the side of the extremist law for not being popular?

But he was big, large, huge, strong, and beautiful. Would you want someone to torture you for those qualities?

Selective empathy is the coward's emotion.

Then to see that justice was served this time brought a sigh of relief that, yes, justice can happen for the roughest torture the modern world has seen live repeatedly.

To hear the brother of George and the mother of Chauvin was to hear two different languages heard but not spoken.

Bandwagon

There are among us some that are righteous, and
some the contrary: we follow divergent paths.
                                          —Sura 72

To lead others towards the good, one
must purify one's own character.
                                          —I Ching

June 8

Most go with a bandwagon
Instead of their light of conscience,
Which we still have inside as gifted by the Divine.
A few can stand alone.
Most think they know everything;
A few need hard evidence.
Too many follow each rich crowd
That follows dual/triple masters.
A few realize the crowds are fake,
Leading to their disaster.
The more we think we know people,
The less we truly know them—
Like classic books, a million sides
To each person's inner traumas,
Layers and layers of pages torn.
In some department, Maya was read
To hide what really happened
As if young minds were imbeciles

Needing no academic experience.
The bandwagons read popular things,
Denying individual histories.
Easy to become mesmerized
By exaggeration's disgraces,
Which went on and on a hundred years ago,
Where Tulsa's hard-earned triumphs
Were forcibly hurled down,
Until evidence was found
By the suffering conscientious.
I was that naive thinker with trust for everyone,
For in good faith was I raised up—
By way of God, not greed.
Most who live for yesterday
Still follow followers of bandwagons—
The few who live for each second's
Grace know reality is calling—
A woman in each society must often stand alone
Instead of going with some bandwagon
Fifting her to break her down
For unjust reasons of their own;
For each society's patriarchy
Fauds only their men and women-following men
As if we women were only backdrops
For men's wondrous successes.
No, win-win for everyone is what the
Mormon preacher taught; win-win in justice for each race
Is what Quran has brought,
That one stands up for justice anywhere
Though it be against oneself or kin.
If any wrongdoing lasts on,
Only God shall carry us home again,
Where good was made by Him.
Amen.

Nature's Guardians

*But in practice, the Muslims accepted that they
had reached the limits of their expansion by
this date, and coexisted amicably with the non-
Muslim world. The Quran does not sanctify
warfare. It develops the notion of a just war
of self-defense to protect decent values, but
condemns killing and aggression. Furthermore,
once the Arabs had left the peninsula, they
found that nearly everybody belonged to the
ahl-al-kitab, the People of the Book, who had
received authentic scriptures from God. They
were not, therefore, forced to convert to Islam;
indeed, until the middle of the eighth century,
conversion was not encouraged. The Muslims
assumed that Islam was a religion for the
descendants of Ismail, as judaism was the faith
of the sons of Isaac. Arab tribesman had always
extended protection to weaker clients (mawali).*
　　　　　　　—Karen Armstrong, *Islam: A
　　　　　　　Short History* (p. 30)

*A person's heart plans his way, but
the Lord determines his steps.*
　　　　　　　—Proverbs 16:9

June 10

A ladybug comes on my handkerchief after walking,
Reaching home (Is this an angel visiting from Heaven?).
It does not harm, having a charming beauty of its own,
Moving along God's wondrous natural path,
Adding joy to the morning,
Red skin like tomato, black or brown tattoos all over.
A redbird flies from branch to branch
In nature's splendid celebrations.
Then there was the other *Lady Bird Johnson*
From here in Texas, making room in her nature
For all in her city life's cavalcade,
Wandering on nomadically
When she could have been playing charming First Lady,
Dressing up for high formalities, following along.
Lady Bird visiting me in my dream as a dream guest?
So as I was taught by gentle ones at home,
Place nature's guardians back where they belong.
I've also met those with huge savior complexes,
Placing nature's guardians in much harm.

The Chasers and the Makers

O Children of Adam! Wear your beautiful apparel
at every time and place of prayer: eat and drink:
but do not waste by excess, for Allah does not
love the wasters. Say: Who has forbidden the
beautiful gifts of Allah, which He has produced
for His servants, and the things, clean and
pure, which He has provided for sustenance?
                                        —Holy Quran

Let those who find not the wherewithal for
marriage keep themselves chaste, until Allah
gives them means out of His Grace. And if any
of your slaves ask for a deed in writing to enable
them to earn their freedom for a certain sum,
given them such a deed, if you know any good in
them; yes, give them something of yourselves out
of the means which Allah has given to you. But
do not force your maids into prostitution when
they desire chastity, in order that you may make
a gain in the goods of this life. [Today, chastity
is almost a forgotten thing and is laughed at
by the majority of the people growing up and
growing wild in a sexually perverted global
society that demeans women and men.]
                                —Sura 24, "The Light"

June 10, 2021

Subhanallah. How violent were the ancient Arabian men before Islam when they misused women for their own gains, as God warns about in the Quran, those of near-Arabian Peninsula who were two-faced about His existence. It was the blessed gender-equitable Prophet who had people stop their devious ways toward women and people of color—rich people who believed God Almighty could free the slaves and marry them or treat the pious people as equals finally. This is why the Prophet was a social reformer rather than a follower of the status quo. He himself married into different tribes, and his blessed wives were not the pretty belles of the towns. Rather, he married to give them dignity.

As the summer breezes blow gently then roughly, I enjoy this moment in time, thinking of the bounties of my Lord, how much He has given human beings, and how much we human beings waste of His bounties.

The twelve pink roses outside stand still compared to all the swaying around them. They stand upright. Maybe that is their prayer to their Maker as we humans try standing upright when societies have taught us to bend too much, forgetting to stand upright to our Maker.

I have never been a chaser. Everything I am or have has been given to me directly by God Almighty. No job did I ever chase, thank God Almighty. No person did I ever chase, no dream, no car, no fancy outfit, no object of worship, except Allah.

And this has been my life's story all along, Alhumdullilah. My very first job came to me by a simple phone call by a good superintendent who also loved all of God's people. His name was Bill Steichmann and was from Illinois.

I had done my second master's degree and was ready to find work, but work found me instead by the grace of Allah.

"Would you like to work for our growing district, Mrs. Salam?" said the generous Bill Steichmann, having done his research on what kinds of teachers and leaders he had wanted for his open-minded district—Cisne High School—and its connecting schools. "We need hardworking, dedicated people who care for all students alike and are quite capable of transformative leadership."

"How did you know, Mr. Bill, that I wanted to be a teacher somewhere good?"

"I just know. Here, we do our research and know people who know people."

"When can I come for the interview, Mr. Bill?"

"As soon as possible. You need to meet with Mr. Michael Pearson and his team in that farming community."

And so I was set on my way, never chasing a dream, but the dream chased me. Guardians of nature do not need to chase anything because the best people, jobs, and dreams come to them without any drama, without any hurting anybody else.

A similar thing happened as I married by choice at the age of... what was it? Twenty-three? Of course, I knew that marriage between two persons or two cultures was supposed to be hard and tough, and no fairytale every existed for 99 percent of people. When I had almost finished my first master's degree in the art of teaching in New Jersey, my mom called me in for a weekend luncheon she was preparing.

"Not another Jane Austen get-together regarding marriage, Ammi? Please, tell me the truth as I am busy writing papers for Dr. Poet, Lahna Diskin, a favorite professor on the campus."

"No, dear, not a Jane Austen marriage interview, just good people from England via Bihar, India, that you might choose to like or not. We have met them through some New Jersey friends."

"Oh, right." I could only imagine at this time, a wonderful poet-engineer named Ahmad, originally from Iran, had proposed to me through an Arkansas sister. They were Shia and very educated, each member of the family. Ahmad was my grandfather's name: "one who gives praise to God Almighty," and it was also the Prophet's name, one of them. I had not even known Ahmad Dastgheib from a poetic family of scientists, as paradoxical as that seems, but Sister Shirin had invited me to dinner in Arkansas when I was trying to rush up and finish my bachelor's in English and Spanish. I was nostalgic from leaving all the Fayetteville family-style friends I had gotten to know through good conversations. When I left Arkansas and visited again, I had understood the great tragedy on campus when a comparative literature great-heart was shot in the chest by his own graduate student.

Destiny could be rough for the greatest people I have met along life's steep path, as Dr. John Locke was loving and kind to everyone, even the young, excessively-ambitious preacher's son, who could not complete his dissertation and had raged against the Buddhist convert, Dr. Locke. In mourning, I knew the millions of good deeds my professor had done ensured that he would be a martyr for the cause of education. When some people are done chasing their dreams, dreams fail before people do. I would rather not chase dreams; I'd let Allah decide my destiny each second of life's way even as I plan as best I can for my retirement and children's contentment. The smaller will He has instilled within my conscience is enough for me to be curious of life's voyages—physical and spiritual, but I am grateful for each venture and each stop on the voyage back to Him.

I was blessed to never have dated or "gone wild" toward anyone as I strictly followed the teachings of the Prophet even as a modern young woman. Sure, I wore my overalls, dungarees, and flannel shirts, but I could never see myself dating, even cheating my parents or lying to them, as many girls had done in my generation in the East Coast. Many also followed the Prophet's way (peace be upon him) and stayed pure and true to his guidelines about chastity until marriage.

Anyway, it's a long story:

I had said no to the Dastgheib family's invitation for marriage because they were very conservative, and most of the women had worn burqas and did not believe that women should hold serious jobs for a long time. They were the kindest people, however, and more civilized in mannerisms than I had known anyone as a family. But I could not see myself traveling permanently to Iran and wearing a chador for the rest of my life at the time. Maybe today I am a different person. Who knows? This marriage may not work out between a semimodern person of feminist leanings and a semitraditional person of conservative leanings in beautiful Iran, advised my counselor—Dad. Although, in retrospect, there are both feminist Muslims in

Iran and excellent modern women of the sciences and arts who have brought joy and introspection to the Islamic arts.

Meanwhile, back in New Jersey, my mom could not be said no to easily. She was as loving and stubborn as the best of moms and only wanted the best for me. So, having an intuition that this would end up being another Jane Austen-style interview, I went along home, dressing up in my version of polite *salwar kameez*: a burgundy-colored outfit with modernistic flowers like a painting; and I wore Ammi's favorite scarf—a dotted floral black-and-red shawl, thin and soft, draping my frontal area with a certain modesty but not too much. Apparently, my future husband, Khursheed, had noticed that outfit on me, though I had rushed to find the first thing I could find from my closet.

After the Jane Austen-style family interview, we two were asked by the elders to go into another room to discuss our tastes in life, our goals, and our interests. I had done enough damage to the group by being so blunt with my father-in-law about where women should stand in society and how much progress we Muslim women needed to make so that we could truly follow the Prophet's way. And I also gave Dr. Abdus Salam, a doctor from Normanton, England, much reason to detest me as much as possible: at each comment he made about world history, I had to argue with him and give him a few supporting facts, for which he was not prepared.

One of them was the history of Spain, apparently a favorite topic of his. Later, I learned from his son that Dr. Salam had many reservations about having me as a future daughter-in-law. He had thought, apparently, that the great Syed Jafar Imam's granddaughter was supposed to be complacent, quiet all the time, and demure as women are "expected to be."

Apparently, this was also what my husband liked about me: that I could speak my mind at ease with supporting facts whether people liked it or not. This, too, would be the story of my life.

After our informal discussions and time away from the family room where Ammi had served her well-known cuisine as a buffet and the teas and desserts she was known for, the other side had decided on me (even with my apparent difficulties). My sister-in-law liked me first, and my mother-in-law, a most peaceful and pious lady of joy and wisdom and traditional education, also liked me as much as my family connections to the Imam family, known for law, education, and justice as minorities in India who had made a great difference in the province of Bihar.

"So are you ready for marriage?" my father asked jokingly.

"Ready? What do you mean? Who can ever be ready for marriage?"

"They're a very nice family, and you got along with them, I noticed," said my mother.

"Do we marry anybody we get along with permanently? Sometimes the very qualities we loved about a person when we first met them are the same qualities that irritate us when we get to know them better!"

Nevertheless, we persevere in our struggle to become better partners and parents for the sake of God. Marriage is an honorary contract between two people who believe in similar things and similar values, beta. I don't remember which wise parent said that.

All comes in time, and people work on getting along with anybody. "Everything in life requires hard work," said someone else in the family. "Everybody is a mystery to be solved," said another cousin.

And it was set. I had liked my blue-suited, handsome future husband, Khursheed, and I found him talkative and amiable. Intellect mattered to me, and he was educated with polite manners. Ele said he liked me the first time he met me, though they were almost close to commitment in Canada somewhere before me. I wasn't pressured about making the right impression, and so I felt free to be myself and didn't even wear much makeup.

They had traveled far and wide to find the right person for their precious son, Khursheed. We, on the other hand, did not bother looking for anyone. We only had faith in Allah. And some of us had faith in marriage too after an education even though we did not date or do the modern things many women seemed to be doing (to their own line of disappointments).

Khursheed has been an amazing son-in-law even if sometimes, I had wished that he chose to develop a broader palette on the emo-

112

tional spectrum as the arts we choose to design our works from. Yet Khursheed has been a stoic example for me about one's work ethic and perseverance, no matter what is going on in the news. He does not let his emotional or intellectual sensitivity bog him down. I wish I did not get so tuned in to the media discussions that go on and on and instead, like Khursheed, could understand deeply that both sides have their flaws—great flaws that hinder democracy. But I allow my personal experiences to move me.

He was actively involved in my parents' best and worse times, taking care of them in the hospitals and taking care of my mom when she had dementia for eleven years. He guided me into becoming a stronger, more resilient, self-dependent woman who depended on him as my family man. This took me a long time to understand. We did not always get along perfectly as we were two different nations under one God. We had two opposite ways of doing and being everything we needed to be to make our blessed family survive and thrive at discordant times. I was more Eastern in my otherness, and he was more Westernized in his British Indian-ness, though, on the surface, our family friends saw me as the Westernized one.

I will always be grateful for my choice in my husband and partner because I could not have found anyone on my own more nearly perfect for me than the man I chose and said yes to, to be my husband. This great blessing gave me life's many opportunities to become who I wanted to be and have fruitful, sacred spaces as well as sacred times together. Ameen.

I was leaning on my Pakistani–New Jersey side of etiquette: be tough yet graceful and meek, be blunt yet strong, and be dignified though rough sometimes. He was leaning on his British Indian side: conservative yet liberal, unaware of race politics, aware of financial causes in politics, and unaware of class hierarchies yet aware of his desire to flow with the system. I, on the other hand, was too aware of systemic hierarchies everywhere and was always leaning on social equality and interpersonal spirituality (as our Prophet did) and my modern heroes in colleges: Dr. Lahna Diskin, Superintendent Bill Steichmann, Dr. Irving Rothman, Dr. Taylor from Illinois State University, Dr. Peter Gingiss, Mrs. Reigeitzz, Mrs. Claire Weimmer,

Mrs. Szarchyz, Shannon, Mrs. Kerwin Sheena, Mr. Steven Crossen, Mr. Alex Hinn, Bernadette, Mr. Nadeau, Ms. Christie A., Auntie Shahaba Imam, Yasmin Roohi Zafar, Mrs. Rosemary McGrory, Dr. John Locke, Hamid Reza Karim, Hasbunnisa Imam Karim, Mrs. Kathie Kiklas, Ms. Janice Reed, Sisters Jaishiri and Sonia Kaur, Sisters Shama and (student) Sarah Rose Hasan, Baby Baji, Dr. Neaz Ahmad, Sisters Saboohi and Annette, the DUA team of spiritual leaders, Cousins Askari and Suboohi, Dr. Masood and Asra Khan, Emm Salam, Sahel Salam, Mariam Salam, Mr. George Hopper, Dr. Michael Worthy, family members I do not get to see, and a few other deeply conscientious souls who could be global family and who understood the bridges to be made by good souls who love all of God's people—bridges not broken nor walls made high by selfish protocols based on class hierarchies.

My views have led me to success and failure by the grace of God in His timing. My husband's divergent views have also led him to his success by the grace of God. The key in this family's learning is to never give up on each other for the higher sake of Almighty's loving mercy even when people try to tear us apart.

Yet how much have I grown in the diversity of our family? Diversity, as many people know, comes not from one's skin color but from one's ethics, ways of being, and raison d'etre. And I will always love my husband and be true to him as Allah's plan has unfolded into me.

Dreams came to me from Allah. I was grateful not to be a chaser but a maker of beautiful moments. I was meant to be a maker of poignant days, and no amount of people's habit of chasing after butterflies would keep me from my goals.

In asking my Maker's help for every single thing—knowledge and wisdom—I must still be aware and practice awareness every step of the way: the awareness of silence and the awareness of stillness amid all the chaotic moments the world imparts to us. Being cautious of our egotistic self does not mean that we are unable to take small risks in life; it is simply that going in the path of God allows one greater freedom to err on the side of His trust rather than err on the side of human beings. Human beings make quick choices with long-term impacts. God gives us long-term impacts with His short teachings, which we can follow or discard. The choice is up to us.

I have always been conscious that a benevolent presence—God, not a fascist dictator, is watching me and all the watchers who watch people. As He teaches us impatient humans in Sura 50, "It was We who created man, and we know what dark suggestions his soul makes to him: for We are nearer to him than his own jugular vein. Behold, two watchful angels appointed to record his doings—one sitting on the right [shoulder] and one on the left. Not a word does he utter but there is a watcher by him, ready to note it." And those of us whose lives are built on words, what we say and do, our thoughts and actions both, matter deeply all the time. Yes, I'd rather err on the side of the Divine than on human intellect; one is sturdy and true, the other, faulty and directionless. And err in judgment we must, as humans we are. Never the devilish imp and never the angel disguised as devil, only human with just enough pride in being of the human race, gravitating back to the Divine, but not too much. For in pride, people fall forever, farther than their own waysides.

As I write this, staring leisurely out the window at the green grass and some plants growing where they will, my dear husband brings me a cup of soup—vegetarian tomato—and our favorite pistachio bread. He has much on his mind yet still makes time to think of me, though I am not working and could be preparing his lunch instead. I walk joyfully with new friends who seem to be old souls of the world's rich traditions, and my husband massages my feet, though I could be doing more massages for him as he lets me not have to worry for his griefs. These new friends seem to know much about teaching, counseling, learning, and the mercy of God. Meeting them seems to have been destined for me when I had begun to lose hope from local people who happened to love the state and nation. It was as if I were finding out again that God Almighty truly does love all people who do good on earth, and perhaps He may want people in all situations to "get to know one another, and not despise one another" (as the frightening mobs had taught me in my shock-learning for years after my ordeal).

How far we have come through the teachings of each other over decades of not letting ourselves go, how far we have grown from not falling into the wells of our egos (rage, fear, worry, mistrust, betrayal, etc.), and letting Allah help us up each time we fall down for however long He deems it necessary—what an impeccable feeling to be alive.
Ameen.

The Precious Hummingbird

*The camel driver understood what the boy was
saying. He knew that any given thing on the face of
the earth could reveal the history of all things. One
could open a book to any page, or look at a person's
hand; one could turn a card, or watch the flight of
birds...whatever the thing observed, one could find
a connection with his experience of the moment.*
—Paulo Coelho, *The Alchemist*

June 19, 20201

Two elements we teachers and writers in today's chaotic times
need in plenty are serendipity and synchronicity, often by the grace
of God. We need to cultivate these ingredients within ourselves to
persevere in the toughest fields of all: whose societal benefit few can
see in writing and teaching when few believe in our works, few offer
support, and even fewer care for our connections (spiritual and emo-
tive-intellectual) with our learners and audiences?

To facilitate a fulfilling learning experience, both learner and
teacher, audiences and writers, may need to work collaboratively
whenever possible. *Not one member is superior to the other, and not
one can shine without the* other. However, the spaces of teaching and
writing are sacred, as sacred as the natural environment given to us by
the Divine Intellect. Once we invade one another's teaching spaces or
put one another down (instead of raising our consciousness toward
all learners and all learning), then we have transgressed what teachers
and writers are best at: creating harmony inside cacophony.

That comes to kiss the new bud rose
Another treasure to watch from the window
Nature's moving pictures
With everything that has soul
How orderly the universe
How spontaneous its soul
Balance in moderation
Gracing the afternoon with its fleeting presence
As time itself
We learn from the
Smallest of beings—a hummingbird appears,
equally blessed in life's
Cyclical growth and renewal—
As long as we don't let ourselves transgress
Our ways of obeying our Maker
Or share divinely inspired gifts of memory and language
We learned somewhere for the sake of knowing
In an ordered sponsorship by the One who sponsors one and all.
Ameen.

Today I honor (again) my blessed parents, who taught me all that I needed to know and more for survival in this realm; no wonder I still converse with them when they (seem to) visit in pastoral dreams. Ameen.

> Isa speaks, Peace be upon him; "And He has made me kind to my mother, and not overbearing or miserable. She pointed to the babe. They said: "How can we talk to one who is a child in the cradle?" He said: "I am indeed a servant of Allah." (Sura Maryam)

I believe that we are all trying to be in tune with our highest purpose since we were born, and each precious child has a sacred purpose on earth unless the child is taught to transgress his or her sacred purpose by doing wicked deeds to people.

Good parents, like elders, our closest family members, guide us, humor us, and remind us when we need guidance in all of our diverse ways and traditions, especially if we are faltering (as my blessed cousins, Dr. N. and T.). They help us keep the path of peace instead of turbulence.

Guides are not dictators, nor do they judge everything about us all the time nor place us in mental "prisons." That is God's job—to judge between our conduct and intentions. *In loco parentis*, for me, has worked the same way while teaching fellow people's children. Teachers cannot and should not take away the students' own traditions and expectations of what they have learned is good conduct. This is where we need to be flexible in understanding a variety of discourses and traditions of excellence through hard work and ethics, cultivated by all people when they align their values, intentions, and work products. Anyone can be in his or her element, as my father called it, when alignment is set between what one wants to achieve and what one's actual values are. No alignment, no achievement, in the honest sense. If we do not put emphasis on the sacredness of each person in the family or class, then we may be the next ones guilty of practicing favoritism or nepotism to the detriment of the whole child.

Like the redbird that steadies itself on man-made instruments, balancing its entire small body on a large structure, we teachers and parents might choose to steady ourselves and not transgress boundaries established by the Divine Authority given in all holy books that we have read. Too rough? We may lose the child/student's trust. Too easygoing? We may let the child transgress into dangerous waters. My cousin reads the picture of the redbird (in my photo collection) balancing itself on the iron platform, and he simultaneously recites the poem that came to me while watching the redbird's carefree movements in perfect balance.

Balance is what we seek as teachers, and teachers at home as one's first parents are one's essential teachers. No one knows except by hope and fervent prayers how, what, and who our children will become. If we stop caring and leave everything to *que sera sera*, then we have already given up—God forbid. Sometimes when we think our children are done listening to us, they may still be listening to what we say and what we don't say, what we advise and what we don't advise.

It is not my job to make careless judgments between students in classes. I could never be a dictator, nor would I want to be someone who pounds her authority, her way of life, or her viewpoints (except for universal values of good and bad conduct), even dressed as "friendliness," into young people's heads. I was grateful to have had many, many life choices when I lived in my parents' house. Maybe this is why I did not deviate or rebel from their sensible teachings with freedom but not freedom in excess.

In many marriages (as in ours), when the parents (we two) are not always aligned in their/our parenting styles, the children are not always aligned with their values and work ethic. This is similar to schools in which the administration is not aligned to their own said values, and so the students lose out and become misaligned and disengaged from their own active learning with broader, long-term goals.

Freedom in the classroom is like freedom learned at home: allow people to do things their ways as long as the objectives are meeting the larger criteria for success and contentment over instant success and shortcuts into fleeting happiness.

This requires the mind's flexibility as muscles are trained to become flexible over time, not constrained. Being a Democrat, Republican, or a middle-ground person has nothing to do with the success of one's students/children at home.

This freedom, with enough guidance to sustain them, is what I wish to pass on to my own children.

When they need something wonderful to rely on, there is God. In God I trust myself fully.

Without God, I am nothing. With God Almighty, I can be anything. The essence of any God-conscious parenting (or teaching) is found in a pithy *I Ching* statement: "To lead others toward the good, one must purify one's own character." And my blessed parents were always purifying their own characters before telling us what to do or how to do it.

Alignment

June 21, 2021

I still have to make you proud of me,
Though I've suffered more than the joy
You knew in me.
After praising Allah as much as often,
I want to be prepared should I meet you again.
The hummingbird comes to kiss the rose,
The redbird walks on awkward terrain,
And here I dream of all that you taught—
How I took you for granted back then.
Whatever I was, whatever I thought,
Whatever I felt, whatever I fought,
You inspired me. Your love kept me going.
Both of you form a fortress made
Of joy, conforming
To one Allah, who gave me birth
Through you, in all the ways
Parents can take a listless babe
And make her real,
Make her feel and know
From whence knowledge came, earthly knowledge and
Knowledge in many forms beyond the human race.
Ameen.

May Allah give you continuous Jannah in the highest realm,
and may He continue to give Khursheed's parents the highest Jannah

within His peace and eternal gardens until we meet again, inshallah. And forgive us parents here on earth who are still struggling with teaching each child without ever ignoring anyone.

Manhattan Rain

To be grateful to our fathers of thought and inspiration without worshiping them—this brings renewed joy in our lives.

As Whitman is our literary father, even today, in the grime of a polarized clime, so are our ancestral (literary) fathers who gave us the inspiration to keep going despite all odds in this polarized society. How much Walt Whitman enjoyed people—the odd works they do, their varied lives, their free-spirited contributions to communities of all kinds. I would read so many poems and essays by Whitman and many other poets with my dad in those early Saturday mornings after he'd make breakfast for us when our mom was resting. New York—Mannahatta, as the natives called it and as Whitman called it—was that place one could visit anytime and see its bustling, care-free energy. As Whitman recollects, so I read him again:

> Numberless crowded streets, high growths
> of iron, slender, strong, light, splendidly uprising
> toward clear skies,
>   Tides swift and ample, well-loved by me,
> toward sundown, The flowing sea-currents, the
> little islands, larger adjoining islands, the heights,
> the villas,
>   The countless masts, the white shore-steam-
> ers, the lighters, the ferry-boats, the black
> sea-steamers, well-modeled,
>   The down-town streets, the jobber's houses
> of business, the houses of business of the ship-mer-
> chants and money-brokers, the river-streets,

Immigrants arriving, fifteen or twenty thousand in a week,

The carts hauling goods, the many races of drivers of horses, the brown-faced sailors,

The summer air, the bright sun shining, and the sailing clouds aloft,

The winter snows, the sleigh-bells, the broken ice in the river,

Passing along up or down with the flood-tide or ebb-tide, The mechanics of the city, the masters, well-formed, beautiful-faced, looking you straight in the eyes,

Trotters thronged, vehicles, Broadway, the women, the shops and the shows,

A million people—manners free and superb—open voices—Hospitality—the most courageous and friendly young men, City of hurried and sparkling waters! City of spires and masts! City nested in bays! My city!" (Walt Whitman, *Mannahatta*)

Whitman brings out the idealist in all of us. When Whitman says "my city," that *my* is a universal *my*, reminding us of our collective eye enjoying the surreal beauty of New York, where everyone can be one body with diversity and *joie de vivre*, celebrating themselves while celebrating fellow others simultaneously.

This is my favorite aspect of Walt Whitman, a true American whose calling was to understand, not just be understood, as many people of today desire without much luck. No one will ever be truly understood when intentions are not right with the viewers or objectify persons who cannot even understand themselves.

When we find joy in our own being, as our Maker made us, and as we accept His making within us, then and only then can we find joy in observing a fellowship of others around us. Then we can find vivacity within ourselves as we see a bird, a tree, and not all Supermen or Superwomen among us. Some of us do not wish to be Superman or Superwoman. We simply exist and enjoy each moment of existence, accepting all human emotions that come with that existence.

This is what my father taught me as well in all the moments I chose spontaneously to visit local museums with him or have the Polish pierogi, Jewish bagels, or Italian pizzas with coffee at weird hours. Not everyone wanted to go on spontaneous trips, and most family members preferred getting ready or preparing way in advance. For me, it didn't matter what homework assignments I had to do or what clothes were not pristine enough for any trip. I could capture the moment with ease and visit the city with the most educated person I had known who could talk science one minute and philosophy the next minute and talk to the local car shop owner, mechanics, or any immigrant from anywhere as much as the locals.

For an introverted person verging on ambiversion, it was all right. This ambiversion of my dad's helped me understand people during my teaching years, and it never mattered where anyone came from, what their social position was, or what their personality proclivities were.

People study Whitman for his style and learn from his techniques. Young writers often want to emulate his craft, but his craft was pure genius that even the Americans took years to understand while the British gained understanding of Whitman quite before Whitman's own countryfolk.

But I study Whitman for his personality. I am interested in his connections with nature, every aspect of his humanity, and every aspect of his drunken joy (ecstasy with human potentiality), which few human beings had understood except for people such as Hafiz, Rumi, or Shakespeare.

It is better to understand than be understood. What affects misunderstanding, however, is when people who don't seek to know themselves seek to find puzzlement in others' ways of being. This is a boundary that seekers cross over to understand the "other" within ourselves.

As it rained in Manhattan many, many decades ago, I reminisced about our trips, family trips, and dad trips to Manhattan. I'm not sure how old I was, but the moment was ageless.

Again, it rains here in Manhattan, where puddles form on the wet concrete. The street by the Fine Arts building—here I took the bus to meet Akka. I was participating in the National Conference of Christians and Jews as my English teacher, Mrs. McGrory, wanted me to. We met in a bagel shop near that universal museum where everyone's art mattered. He wondered sardonically why I had been selected to go to this meeting when *Judeo-Christian* did not have the third tag: *Islamic.*

Of course, I ignored the invitation for a little while. Why was I selected to go to this meeting? And what would I have to say in front of these great debaters of diverse social issues? I was introspective but still not a socialite. Apparently, Mrs. McGrory had believed I had much to contribute based on the timed writings and class presentations she had us do from time to time.

Well, the bagels and coffee with extra Philadelphia cream cheese were yummy. I don't remember how many we had as we both liked to eat as though eating itself were an art form! We thanked the Jewish owners of the bagel shop and came upon a discussion of Maimonides and his concept of virtues.

The bagels were the gift of the Jews or the Poles to New York City. My dad's lessons on cultures and traditions and his various wisdom from different cultures never ceased to become boring to me, even as a young person.

Later, much later, we'd share other conversations—when he was seventy-three or so—about what Sarah Palin had to say about Barack Obama and what Barack had to say about Senator McCain. It was enough to be aware of politics, but that was enough for me as I did not consider myself a political person; later, First Lady Michele Obama would say this too. She declined a fanatical interest in the politics of the day, and I understood her position as a mom, a wife, and a loyal family member.

The television noise, the excess noise anywhere—those were what I detested while we three sisters were growing up. I could watch television for small periods of time, shows such as *General Hospital* after school or *The Waltons* with Ammi, but just enough. Not too much, as excess of anything would give me headaches even back then.

Before speaking in that Manhattan group, I recall Akka's words that served as a source of extra information that I had not yet studied on my own. High school speakers usually do not read tons of information on world religions and cultures due to lack of time or lack of interest. For me, it was a lack of time due to many school assignments at any given time, which was the reason I did not read up as much as I'd have liked to in those days. Yet he was my thought advisor whose world knowledge was as broad as an encyclopedia. Any question or topic? He'd have it at the top of his head even as he lay dying in the hospital; his reading and historical memory was accurate as Ammi's used to be before the young doctor carelessly put extra anesthesia in her system as she was getting a woman's surgery, causing her to have the dementia of a diseased person—not anticipated in the family. My father, too much of a pacifist, did not press a lawsuit on the young doctor, as practical relatives advised. He had said, "What would money do when such an injustice happened due to carelessness?" Nothing would alter her state, although he did file complaints on the young doctor. The will of God must have some rationale, he tried to remind himself as he knew she would not be herself again. Yet he continued taking care of her, nourishing her spirit with loving devotion, taking her for walks, talking to her as though nothing had happened, and making the cuisines that she had made for him to the best of his ability.

I did not visit them as much as I could have and spent long, long hours concentrating on students' letters of recommendation and their timed writings and portfolios for their future's sake (more than for Allah's sake), and maybe this is why part of my punishment came from Allah. Maybe I could have spent time with the parents who sacrificed everything for selfish me: for the person who loved to learn and didn't even know how much I was making in terms of salary because I was too involved in a job that would later turn out to be duplicitous for me. It could be I deserved what I got from the will of Allah for not being as engaged in my parents' later lives as they had always been engaged in my life and my children's lives like saints.

My dad had said on that rainy Manhattan day, "You might apply for a translator job with all of your love for languages maybe for the United Nations or a small company." Whatever I chose to do—even teaching, he supported me emotionally and spiritually 100 percent. It did not matter how simple my job description was as long as I'd make a contribution to my current society as Walt Whitman saw the daily contributors in his society.

"Women, no matter how rich or poor, always need to support themselves," Akka would say. He would have cried to see that the teaching job I walked out on due to harassment in the workplace by mobs was the end of my passion. I will not disappoint him because writing is the cousin of teaching, and teaching is the offshoot of a conscientious contributor to any community in which one lives.

For his sake and for the sake of Allah, I need to be myself still even though I am a sunken version of what and how I used to be due to hate crimes toward me for several decades now.

I am glad I am done with teaching people who do not want to learn anything besides how to get rich. Ameen.

Irrelevant Quotes and Emotional Quips (IQ + EQ)

Travel Sections

Travel is the best teacher.
—William Wordsworth

Contents

1. Public Relations in Puerto Rico 133
2. Lessons from Al-Ghazali 138
3. Defining Spiritual Hygiene 146
4. The Continuity of Religious and Spiritual Life 151
5. Reflections from Al-Ghazali's *The Marvels of the Heart* 158
6. "Whatever Makes You Happy" Goes Pop Psychology 166
7. When Objectification Becomes the Object 173
8. The Price of Everything, the Value of Nothing 178
9. Confronting Our Hypocrisies in an Age of
   Disappointment 182
10. Remembering England in an Age of Trump 188
11. Making Sense Out of Nonsense:
    Too Much Formulaic Writing in Schools? 193
12. Overconsumption of the World Can Cause… 196
13. Carbohydrates and Kind Words 199
14. On Cowboys 203
15. Part of a Recorded Dream while Being Pregnant
    with My Third Blessed Child 205
16. Worldly Religion 214
17. Praying after a Nightmare 216
18. Andalusia 219
19. My Haven on Earth 220
20. On Finding Someone's Old Report Card: Human Natures....223
21. Why Do We Teach Anyway? 225
22. Carrying Our Truth in Our Own Hearts 230
23. When Companies Mess Up Big-Time 235

24. The Choices We Make..237
25. Survivors, All of Us, Until We Don't....................247
26. Our Age-Long Concerns 249
27. The Miraculous Power of Prayer 251

Public Relations in Puerto Rico

My famous poetry professor once told me as he was rushing out of yet another scheduled conference, "The only advice I have for your writing is slow down. You write like a train on fire."

I listened, putting away my yellow pad for notes from the wise-counselor-turned-poet, and asked him, "So does this mean our conference is over?"

"Yes, ma'am. The women in the class always have *lots to talk about.* See you tomorrow."

I did not understand why such a man was even teaching. I had had other famous professors, poets, and playwrights before, but this man was a bigger deal than even others who thought he was such a big deal. Anyone who could write about bathing his elderly, handicapped mother with disgust in his poetry was already someone I had no affinity for. For me and a couple of colleague-friends, the man epitomized misogyny.

So I walked away in my normal way, staring at the halls in the old, rusty English department that I had excitedly entered in the hopes of fulfilling an old dream about learning as much as I possibly could about literature and languages, etymology, and customs. Lucky for me, my true favorite professor, Dr. Irving Rothman, met me in the hallway. He is no longer alive now, and as much as I respected him and Dr. Peter Gingiss, these two fountains of knowledge were nothing like the self-declared big-deals that began popping up like cacti all over the campus in different departments. When humanity ceased serving the bighearted ones, the bighearted ones began downsizing, shrinking their own potential humanity to fit in with the wrecks of society, rushing to win more acclaim or a dollar.

Dr. Rothman and I had a long discussion over coffee about another chapter for my dissertation. He had no issue with spending his valuable time for all students he valued. One time, he even let my ten-year-old son join me in his graduate class for Swift and Johnson studies, assuring my child that whatever he was studying was just as good as what the adults were dissecting. This kind of professorship is heartfelt and rare in today's time, and the less of a big deal someone thinks he is, the more of a big deal they are to me, like Drs. Rothman and Peter Gingiss.

"What does this have to do with Puerto Rico and the travel department?" you might ask. Very little on the surface. But just as Minister Swift would turn circles right in the middle of his analogical lectures, Puerto Rico came to me when I was not ready for my own PR in Puerto Rico.

I was embittered from a long and useless personal defense war against an entire group of angry, violent people whose personal scapegoat I had become before I entered the generous clime of San Juan Airport with my spouse, I was also not ready for such a warm reception from people we hardly knew.

Like the memory of my good professors, who never thought of themselves as big deals, the local Puerto Ricans practiced such refinement that a king would be ashamed of his big-deal-ness.

"Let me get this for you," and, "Let me tell you what's the best hotel and best restaurant and what the locals like during quiet hours," said the young man from San Juan Airport. I saw a colorfully dressed family, hats and all, looking like they had come from Gilligan's Isle to Puerto Rico, the kids rolling their eyes when the family money would come out and speak to the humble service provider.

Still, the young man continued talking to the Gilligan's Isle family as suavely and properly as he did with us. This service could be discounted. And that service could be discounted. I did not understand how many advantages there were in each day of our trip. It was as if the slower and more calmly I spoke the nicer each person became. I was not the person my bigoted, famous poet-professor had brazenly critiqued on being too "fast" like a "train on fire." I was relaxed in a relaxed, joyful atmosphere in every single place I went—from the

Isla Verde beach to the bistec-specialty restaurants to the rock-on-a-hill outing to the Embassy Suites by Hilton, where I met another delicious converses a sister-seeming from Puerto Rico, reminding me of my first college roommate, another fine Puerto Rican gal named Julie, with whom I had shared countless moments of family time.

No matter what tacky outfit I wore (I am not known for my sense of style or finesse, but I do select interesting color combinations that my husband is not too fond of) and however my body looked as I was shopping or walking, no one would be rude. Each person made sure to pronounce my name accurately and my husband's name with equal honor from the restaurants to the hotels. Not all people there were made of money, but all people had a sense of honor and duty. It was strange, indeed, to be treated so nicely just two and a half years ago—July, 2018—when even an old job set would purposely mispronounce my name even after working with me for over twenty years! Puerto Rico was a refreshing course I took as God gave me another opportunity to see good Christians and other faiths working and living together without hating each other.

The trip reminded me perfectly of this line in the Quran that I repeat like a mantra to my husband and family whenever they appreciate something weird from Mr. Trump: "We have created you from nations and tribes so that you may get to know one another, and not despise one another, and to test you to see which ones of you are virtuous and pious in conduct." Puerto Rico taught me not to judge large groups of people the way I was misjudged due to my religion and looks by misogynists of America (there must be a club or cult, I am sure), and Puerto Rico gave me a refresher course on appreciating everyone for their individual souls and manners as Professors Rothman and Gingiss appreciated me just as I was: not perfect but a worthy person to be respected as much as anyone else.

My family was becoming scared for me as I had taken an almost about-face from the vagaries of impudence coming in my direction, almost making me as blind and prejudiced as the many misogynistic racists I had met, trying to act better than anyone else. Puerto Rico, as a course, taught me to look back on the bright side as I used to do—the original me, free from the sins that I had been around for too long.

It took a rich place in the soul to talk back to the lack of riches in America in her broken soul that she could not embrace all people at any given time. Puerto *Rico* (Rich Port), in my mind, had become the gem of America no matter how little attention the fancy, rich, spoiled people had given her after natural disasters as the government gave to Louisiana. But who's comparing, really? Vivian, at the Embassy Suites, who had joined my husband and me for breakfast just for fun, shared how much the hurricanes and tornadoes had done to her house with no help from the government. Still, the grace and beauty of her presence could warm the much-traveled, cold hearts so that we had the time.

"I'm telling you, Vivian, I wasn't expecting such friendly and loving people everywhere I visited, and I'm sorry that I am leaving."

"We should get each other's numbers, since we can't stop talking to each other. My husband's on the other side of this hotel. Otherwise, I'd ask him to come join in. Maybe it's that we've been through a lot here, doing everything on our own with no help from authorities. And so people can become cold, or they can stay warm from inside out."

"I prefer the warmth here to any place I have recently traveled in the States. Wish I could stay," I told her.

"We have to leave tomorrow, so don't get too comfortable," my husband, the pragmatist, joined in. Vivian smiled. And we all exchanged a final smile as if that's what we met up for: to join in on long smiles and longer conversations for no reason related to money or status.

Only God knows how people are taught to treat one of their own: Puerto Rico. Wordsworth, in his ramblings on *Lines Composed a Few Miles Above Tintern Abbey*, once wrote that "the best portion of a good man's life, his little, nameless, unremembered acts of kindness and of love." The key word here is *unremembered*. And when I visited Wordsworth and Coleridge's walking areas in England's lush green for our honeymoon twenty-eight years ago, I also remembered in that atmosphere the same kind of human friendliness, the affinity for all human nature that decorates humanity as all the colors that nature wears. Emerson knew this—*the colors that nature wears*, yet how far we Americans are from Emerson and Wordsworth's transcendental knowing of life beyond ourselves. In Puerto Rico, this feature of human experience was still preserved in 2018.

After all, when are we, mere human beings, at a big deal in our lives? When we unknowingly are treating each person we meet or speak to as if they were one of our own.

Lessons from Al-Ghazali

February 2, 2021

In *Marvels of the Heart*[1] Al-Ghazali discusses keeping ourselves as clean and decent as possible to keep demonic presences away from the human heart that want to be near Allah:

> You may say, "But how can Satan appear to some men and not to others?" If one sees his form, is it his real form, or is it an image in which Satan appears to him? If it is his real form, how is it that he is seen in different forms? How can he be seen in two places and in two forms at the same time in such a way that two people see him in two different forms? Know that the angel and demon each have two forms from which are their real forms. These are not perceived by natural sight, save only by the illumination of the prophetic office.
>
> The Prophet only saw Jibril, may the best of blessings and peace be upon him, in his true form on two occasions. Once the Prophet asked him to show himself to him in his real form, and Jibril appointed for him a place, Baqi. He appeared to him at Hira and filled the whole horizon from

---

[1]   Al-Ghazali, *The Marvels of the Heart, Book 21: The Revival of the Religious Sciences*, translated from the Arabic with an introduction and notes by Walter James Skellie with a foreword by T.J. Winter (49 Mockingbird Valley Drive, Louisville, Kentucky 40207, USA: Fons Vitae, 2010), ISBN: 978-1-887752-31-2.

East to West. He saw him again in his true form the night of the Heavenly Journey (al-miraj), at the lote tree of the boundary. But for the most part he saw him in the form of a man. He used to see him in the form of Dihya al-Kalbi, who was a man of goodly countenance. For the most part he [the spiritual being: angel or demon] unveils an image of his form to the people of unveiling (ahl al-mukashafa) and possessors of hearts (arbab al-qulub); and thus he appears to one of them while he is awake, and this man will see him with his eye and hear his speech with his ear. This will take the place of his real-form.

In like manner he is revealed to a majority of good men during sleep. Revelation during waking hours is made only to one who has attained such a high rank that the occupation of his senses with the things of this world does not prevent the revelation which comes in sleep, so he sees while awake what another sees during sleep. It is also related on the authority of Umar b. Abd al-Aziz, may God have mercy on him, that a man asked his Lord to show him the place Satan occupies in relation to the heart of man. He saw in his sleep a man's body, which was like crystal, and the inside of it was visible from without. He saw Satan in the form of a frog sitting on the left shoulder [a dream similar to mine, in which I saw bigger satanic figures holding the smaller satanic figures, who seemed like bulging frogs in the pockets of certain rich, evil people with demonic hearts; may Allah keep such people away from the righteous across all Faiths, Ameen] between the shoulder and the ear, and he had a long and thin proboscis which he had put in through the left shoulder into the heart in order to make evil promptings to it. [As the Quran says, we should avoid the "whispering ones"—those who make people follow evil ways.] Whenever [the man] made mention of God the Exalted, Satan withdrew.

This very same thing is sometimes seen in waking hours, for some of the people of unveiling have seen Satan in the form of a dog reclining on a carcass and inviting men to it. [This image reminds me of Hitler and Goebbels with their big dogs and their hatred of fellow human beings they thought different from the "superior" but spiritually, perhaps, on the path toward martyrdom toward God.] The carcass represents this lower world [Islam is cognizant of many worlds parallel and better than this world]. This is like observing his real form. For, of necessity, reality must appear in the heart from that side of it which is turned toward the world of spirits. Then its influence shines upon the side that is turned toward the visible material world, for the two sides are connected, the one with the other.

We have already explained that the heart has two sides. One of them is turned toward the world of the Unseen, which is the place of entrance of inspiration, both general (Ilham), and prophetic (Wahy). Another side is turned toward the world of the sense [the commercials people are absorbed by]; and that which appears of this world in the side toward the world of sense is only an imagined form, for the world of sense is entirely subject to imaginative reproduction [we see this in technology, very often deceptive]... But the form produced in the imagination by the illuminating effect of the world of spirits upon the inner secret hearts cannot but reflect accurately their qualities and correspond to them. For

140

the form in the world of spirits follows the true characteristics and corresponds to it. So it is not strange that the hideous reality is not seen, save in a hideous form. Thus, Satan is seen in the form of a dog, a frog, a pig, and so on. The angel is seen in a beautiful form, and this form is an indication of the ideal realities and a true reflection of them. [My dreams of good, hardworking souls seemed to be in a greener, happier reality beyond this reality, such as my pious Jewish professor and my parents on different dream occasions.] Therefore, the monkey or pig seen in sleep indicates some hideous likeness while a sheep indicates a man of integrity [remember that sociopaths and other evil-following creatures often paint others with what they really are in their hidden knowledge of themselves, doing evil deeds, which psychology calls projecting one's emotions onto others who seem to bring out the "demon" from among themselves]. From thinkers' readings into the original Bible, we also know that Jesus, peace be upon him, came to the "lost sheep of Israel," and there were many who wanted to do good on earth, despite the evil people around them. Thus it is with all the categories of dreams and their interpretation.

These are strange mysteries, and they belong to the wonders of the heart. It is not fitting to mention them in this book on the knowledge of proper conduct. But the intent is that you shall believe that Satan is revealed to possessors of hearts, and so also the angel, sometimes by means of a representation and reflection, such as takes place in sleep, and sometimes in reality. For the most part, revelation is representation by a form that reflects the ideal reality, not the ideal real-

ity itself. The latter is, however, seen by the eye
in genuine eyewitness[ing]. Only the person of
unveiling has this direct sight, not others around
him, as for instance a man asleep. (112–115)

In one of my many learnings from my elder cousins Dr. Neaz
Bhai and Baby Baji Tanveer, I learned to dissect discussions in sober
ways—as if I had to put aside the emotional parts of my nature
first—in order to clinically study the meanings that were being pre-
sented at any discussion table. Through their loving-kindness, deep
and profuse knowledge of human nature, philosophers-like, good
business minds, and the practical parts of Islam, I saw a different
side of the Islam that I had not studied by myself through books
alone. Hence, my short but pithy study of Al-Ghazali began directly
in their library. Their practical wisdom of applying each facet of our
universal Deen allowed me to see my own family life and marriage in
new and intricately beautiful ways—it was as if Allah had given me
angelic yet tough counselors to help me understand the wisdom of
my husband's teachings of the empirical side of life.

Al-Ghazali had allowed himself to distance himself from regular
worldly ways of teaching and lecturing towards direct meditation in
the Way of Allah to make these discoveries during personal study. I
was always inclined toward the spiritual worlds even more than the
epistemological realities of why and how humans do certain things to
certain people. But reading Al-Ghazali at this venture in my life has
proven to be a kind of kinship with his intellectual as well as spiritual
faculties.

At another point in revisiting the profound text of Al-Ghazali,
(the book my cousin lent me while I visited him recently), Ibrahim
b. Adham was asked (Al-Ghazali explains), "Why is it that we suppli-
cate and our petitions are not granted, although the Exalted has said,
"Call upon me, I will answer you"?

He answered, "Because your hearts are dead" (109). To revive
the human heart, the human heart must make severe changes in its
ways of worshiping God, ways of living, ways of treating people, and
not being overconfident about one's own sense of salvation. I found

in my own life experiences the most chaotic people sitting near are the ones who are haughty about their own salvation—people who do not do the works on the way of God, nor do they/fellow humans live clean, decent lives according to their clear guidelines, letting human hands guide them rather than Almighty God himself.

Al-Ghazali's mystic powers have found that there are eight bad habits many people acquire that kill their ability to be close to God:

1. You have known God's right over you but have not done your duty toward Him.
2. You have read the Quran but have not acted according to the limitations it has imposed.
3. You have said, "We love the Messenger of God," but you have not followed his law (Sunna).
4. You have said, "We fear death," but you have not prepared for it (by fearing Allah, doing good works, loving Allah, and not following evil ways on earth by destroying earthlings or nature or any structures out of mischief).
5. The Exalted has said, "Indeed Satan is an enemy to you, so take him as an enemy" (35:6), but you have agreed with him upon acts of disobedience.
6. You have said, "We fear the fire," and constrained your bodies to enter it.
7. You have said, "We love paradise," but have not labored to gain it.
8. When you have risen from your beds, you have cast your faults behind your backs and spread the faults of other men before your faces. You have angered your Lord, so how can He answer your prayers?

As Al-Ghazali closes the chapter on the ways by which Satan enters the heart, he offers the following exemplum on what not to do and how not to live:

> Mujahid, (a dervish) said, 'Iblis (Satan)
> has five sons and has appointed to each one of

them the charge over a certain matter. They are Thabr, al-Awar, Miswat, Dasim, and Zalanbur. Thabr is the master of afflictions who commands destruction, rending of clothes, [see the nudity and skimpy outfits people of Satan wear today], smiting of cheeks, and the claim of the days of ignorance (al-lahiliyya), as in people who despise learning or knowledge of all kinds. Al Awar is the master of adultery who commands thereto and makes it appear beautiful. [Look at how many people do these lewd acts then pretend to be righteous in front of their school crowds.] Miswat is the master of lying. [Look at all the lying politicians and educational administrators who we can see this from far before they commit their heinous acts of deception in front of educators and community members; they think that God is not watching them.] Dasim enters into the relations between a man and his family, accusing them of faults, and making him angry at them. [Look at how many fathers are angry at their own children and home folks, accusing them of not doing such and such while neglecting their own faults; also look at how many times we homemakers, male or female, are making snide remarks to our own family members.] Zalanbur is the master of the marketplace, and by reason of him those in the market continue to be unjust to one another. [How few people follow the guideline "Give just measures to everyone" in today's commercial marketplaces and how many cheat people into giving more money for basic things that should be free or within a certain price range; they also think that the god they don't believe in isn't watching them at all times].

144

Reading Al-Ghazali makes one more cognizant of looking inwardly rather than outwardly and seeing what one can do to make large improvements in how we treat ourselves and our own loved ones. Decent living means treating others even better than how we were treated, for the sake of Allah alone and not for the sake of pleasing the masses (some of whom are followers of God while some are followers of Satan).

1/26/21
Defining Spiritual Hygiene

January 26, 2021

I must admit, there was a time I did not have my own version of spiritual hygiene, and I said whatever it was that was on my tongue—no filter. This habit could make one win many uncanny friends with a few good ones too, which we shall lose if we continue talking without a filter all the time. To decipher between the correct time to be blunt in speech and when not to say anything at all is what *tact* has come to mean for me. I know there are many definitions of *tact* in polite societies of all social codes. But in the long run, an uncontrolled tongue does not serve a person well no matter how noble his or her intentions, especially not in the way of God. We can say all that we want to about being God-conscious people, but verbiage and a few good actions do not make one spiritually clean. And while one works hard at keeping the body and mind clean, the house clean, and the home clean; having clean friendships; and making clean dinners while cleaning up well enough, these habits only begin one's journey in the hygienic realm of human decency.

For example, let's take a not-so-important endeavor in the broken state of national education. The Scrims ' Spelling Bee contest, popular with all children of intellectuals from various educational leanings, expects the children to state and pronounce words that had Nazi underpinnings (if one is aware of Nazi causes that still dare to laugh at the suppressed or oppressed groups, sometimes the oppressed groups turn around and become the suppresser of other oppressed groups instead of the benign warrior for justice for all, which the Quran and the Constitution equally recommend; people can do their own research). The last year's spelling bee words included *Himalayan* and *ignoble* and race-specific words that social Darwinists target as their foes. "He who laughs last laughs loudest [or prays for the other side]" goes the motto about people who scorn others they do not know much about.

In ensuring that young, impressionable students (mine was an award-winning local Muslim Malaysian American student) would have to look up the etymology and word cousins of each Nazi-inspired word against darker/Muslim population groups, the Scrims' Spelling Bee ceased to be an equality-based institute. Every Asian and Muslim intellect (younger generations) noticed this tactic, and in saying the words for the children to spell, I also noticed the agenda behind Scrims' Spelling Bee: malice for others, hatred for others (as was common in the public schools in which I was targeted), and justice for few rather than none. Spiritual hygiene pronounces all people as equals, as the Constitution does, no matter what sensibilities extremist people have from any religion or the nonreligious.

Increasing numbers of people of intellect tend to see through double agendas; they are those who have what Dubois called a double consciousness. As Quranic wisdom teaches any thinker, Allah is always on the side of the oppressed, not the oppressor, which new French philosophers such as Derrida and Foucault are also aware of. (In Trump losing, we saw whose side Allah is on: the oppressed from every creed and every injured party.) Spiritual hygiene takes into account all people, not just those who are not accountable for the success of all people. Who can ever forget the callous phrase iterated by the son-in-law of Mr. Donald J. Trump: "Blacks have to want success"? This lack of spiritual hygiene speaks deeply about that man's philosophy in five words.

I have been raised in a secularly pious home where secular habits mattered just as much as religious habits and where people loved going to work and working from home also, and my school and television environment left me with a cursing tongue (corrected by my parents)—a bad habit that is commonly found even in the best of homes in the New York and New Jersey areas. Even a few of my teachers, though most were gifted with dealing with people of all backgrounds and educational levels, had that cursing and high-temper-color on their lips, sucking out the healing parts of manners from their personalities.

The people I looked up to, from different creeds and social backgrounds, shared one thing in common: the know-how of what to say at the right moment with just the right words and just the right tone, keeping God in mind as the light would grace their faces. Never did such people have a double face inside a working mask that we all (sensible types) choose to wear today while visiting town plazas or doing errands.

Allah tells us in Sura "Repentance" that "doing idle talk" (wasting time with gossip and slander) gets one nowhere in His path and that the tone of one's speech matters very much no matter whom we are addressing. Among political candidates and leaders, one's tone is quite evident in his or her grasp of social (not socialist) manners toward one's fellow human brothers and sisters of all creeds and walks of life. In every family, we have met polite and impolite people, people who are aware of the multiplicities of human life, people who are not yet aware, people who use meek and gentle words, and people who use harsh and oppressive language as part of their makeup. We are all people undergoing transformation.

There are many stories of Jesus, peace be upon him, talking kindly to people from all walks of life. Similarly, the Prophet Muhammad had lived through many conversations with people from the illiterate venue to ladies with bad manners toward men as well as people who willingly called themselves his enemies, which, according to the Quran, could be anyone who denies the existence of Almighty God, who Arabs call Allah. Spiritual hygiene ensures us that we not only get the job done, as the saying goes, but that we are conscious of what we are saying to each person at any given time and that we exist as an equal human being whose actions lead to other people's actions and deeds. By our consistent tones of speech, as every decent English teacher and preacher of any creed knows, we tend to know who is God conscious and who is not. This does not mean I have a problem with humanistic atheists, only with atheists who have lost their sense of common humanity and chose to will their agendas onto believers who have already experienced their cleanliness and cleansing from a higher power and who are working on their tongues being sanitized before their hands are sanitized in front of crowds.

Spiritual hygiene requires of us a transformation from our previous selves, who said anything that was on our minds, into people who are more mindful than ever toward everyone, more generous in spirit than ever before, and more inclusive in all of our agendas, for everyone on earth will have some kind of agenda: from human symmetry in getting along to human chaos in sowing the seeds of discord.

When I listen to President Biden speak these days, his tone, mannerisms, and gentility remind me of people I knew while growing up in this same country: people who are aware of fellow others inside each human's otherness and that we are all equal before God Almighty until He proves us wrong in His eternal time. By contrast, President Trump and too many—not all but too many—of his followers had his similar lack of social tongue control and lack of spiritual hygiene: boastfulness, braggadocio beyond Beowulf, and simplistic hostility without any lived-bit of righteous anger for lack of societal justice for all, leading to peace for all people, not just a few people. "What about those precious peace treaties between America and Middle East nations?" some might ask.

Any rich boaster can make temporal peace with any other rich boaster; treaties are only treaties, not actions, not lasting transactions of devotion between people and all the castes still existing in man-made lands not conscious of God's eternal plans. Already, President Biden, by contrast, is making contact with the dreaded Putin and his stake in America to inform the informants' informers that he, not Russia, not Mother Russia (changing her many forms), is in charge of the American people. And that takes spiritual and social hygiene, which Mr. Putin has not learned of yet.

Still, time will tell. Politicians are still politicians, and they have their own reasons for choosing politics as a field of service. After all, I am aware that the same administration has gone to war and bombed several Muslim lands whose people are still undergoing survival while we became richer for a time. As of now, we in America are undergoing survival by a higher projector of destinies than our own.

Should we choose social and spiritual hygiene toward a personal transformation? Who knows how many people we might affect in our immediate land before we are designated for other lands, as many holy books tell us, the thinking types? Even selective charity and selective empathy (for example, you get an eighty-nine, as my journalist daughter received for being a conscientious reader of all books before research, knowing more than her teacher, while a ninety-one was given to another who read nothing and did no research but was of the same mindset as her talented and smart English teacher, with whom I enjoyed talking with on and off) have gone far out of hand.

At least in teaching, we once knew justice and fairness should come to all learners, which is the first thing we learn from the states of Illinois and New Jersey—my first places to learn about teaching and leading people to lead themselves with fellow others in mind. Ultimately, practicing spiritual hygiene is to cleanse oneself from unjust talking of the other inside a sea of otherness. For, indeed, there will come a time in which we will all be others inside God's sea of otherness, near the First Other, the First Mover. As the Bible says too, and I paraphrase, "Those who are last, may be first; and those, first, last." Only God knows, and not man, where we each are heading.

The Continuity of Religious and Spiritual Life

January 22, 2021

These last few weeks, I, too, learned many things.

And knowledge is still a precious commodity, all kinds of knowledge, despite what crowds used to holler about under the redneck-beat breath in dark gyms where people only worried about their own bodies and how others felt about them and where 24 Hour Fitness, right-wing, wrong radio made me irritated by some of the music I used to love in my days of uninspired inner darkness, even songs I'd have a meaning for that now had no more meaning but Trumpian-illness echoes of "Hey, teacher, we don't need no education" by Pink Floyd. (Again, I'm not against the group, just the song at the age of ignorance, which took excessive pride in being ignorant.) And of course, their right-wing, unrighteous radio stations sang cheap and dirty body songs that I refuse to listen to anymore as having subjected my decent self to indecent environments. Allah took me out of there and the schools that also played many indecent songs that did not focus on the human soul, human understanding, or clean living (while the administration acted out in Trumpian styles of behavior, contrary to what holy books and the Constitution teach people.)

The dream this afternoon was as interesting as yesterday's and yesterday's dreams.

Allah says in the Quran that if we truly try harder, He may speak to us through "screens" of inspiration. I was in a classroom again, and young people with clean hearts were also there. The green-and-gold podium my students had decorated for me was also there; it was a donation from Home Depot for me. I was grateful to that company for always being kind to me as they were much more open-minded that the Barnes and Nobles where I'd spend useless amounts of hard-earned money for books I did not need. The afternoon dream's theme seemed to be that the collective energy of any environment does not matter, that only one's actions and intentions matter to the Highest Power, and that one can be loved by Him but hated by the crowds/ mobs. And that is actually an accomplishment rather than a failure, as we are taught to think. I felt warm and embraced as I woke up, and the green podium was in the background; the students in the background were still learning and earning honest livings—that particular Morley class with many thoughtful individuals whom I knew and felt would achieve great things intellectually, career-wise, and perhaps even spiritually (their way for their own benefit).

Then there was yesterday's dream, which had me touring an old *masjid* that I had my two children attend for a short while until their dad got them out for reasons of his own. Unlike what most ignorant people imagine about mosques and schools related to mosques (as per what an ignorant comment made by a theater teacher who pretended to like or "tolerate" me, saying that apparently, *madrasas* teach students to hate fellow Americans and that Muslim students are better off learning more about Zionism and her way of life), the *masjid* where I was in (Bear Creek) was actually teaching people to respect and cherish all people for the sake of God. And though some teachers and leaders had accents from distinct places while some were local reverts to Islam, the love and care for all people's children were evident in each day's teaching.

The only thing my husband did not seem to like was a Quran teacher who seemed patronizing to him; he did not like my American accent nor my children's American accent when learning to recite Arabic passages. This alone, combined with a disagreement on teaching methods, caused my husband to take my kids out of the program. In those days, I did not question my husband very much and probably would have been better off letting the kids learn more anyway, but I believe that keeping harmony in the home, as much as I am able to, can help lead the environment from the background. But in this dream, I was also reciting certain verses that united people and helped us remember that our higher purpose in life is to go in His way of peace and peaceful resolutions for all people, not just for ourselves (or whomever we considered part of ourselves).

My children's earliest teacher was in the dream. She had motivated them to learn reasoning skills and mathematics and to set realistic expectations with God in mind while I was teaching literature at the community college and high school. She was smiling in the dream and was as busy helping her special education child as usual. She had used her literature degree and education training for my children, and for that I will always be grateful.

In the previous day's dream, Akka had come back to visit me, and he was sitting Indian style on a green grass, as he often did, and was smiling back at me as if I had finally learned to do the right thing and accept each part of my destiny with Allah's mercy in mind. In this dream, people had their separate peace, and each one, their separate space. And space was always healthy for me, even in the classroom, where I made peacekeeping values a normal part of the daily lesson plan for twenty-six years without need of outside intervention from downstairs people, by the grace of God.

Dreams are a vehicle of growth and inspiration, and when society tells us that only the empirical things matter, I know inwardly that this is not true. Our inward life complements our outer life in daily problem-solving—something interviewers who were biased toward me would smile about askance as if I were speaking another language besides established human languages.

Our inward life can also reestablish the said values in the home department. How we practice our separate space and peace sets an example for others in the home department to come to us as necessary but not invade our personal space and time to think. Allah's verse on men not "annoying women" and letting them live as they themselves wish to live reminds me of honoring women's separate peace while establishing their chosen routines.

These last few weeks have also reminded me of the Hindu declaration that Karmic justice does exist at a fundamental level and that what we give to people does return to us in different ways.

If most of our tasks are of good nature toward all people, goodness comes back to us in ways that we cannot list. I disagree with the popular culture ethic that people, especially women, must make many mistakes to be memorable or make history. History in this world is irrelevant because it keeps changing based on "his-stories" of men who like to be in control of women. Since Islam takes man's possessive nature and tames it down into a feminist nature of respecting the person before what she looks like or how she is perceived, the woman is in full control of taking charge of how she wants to be as long as she serves God above all earthly people, which society and the Bible call masters. Quranic wisdom has an addendum to women's treatment toward justice just as the Constitution has addendums to downtrodden people's justice with regard for justice for all. This is why we are fortunate to live in a country that has law and order of the highest kind, which we human beings of wisdom should not take for granted, pretending to play God (for as we have learning in human histories, even "his-stories" from men's point of view). When we try playing God, God's wrath, not mercy, comes upon us. This I promise from my intuitive and real-life sense.

If most of our tasks are of possessive, obsessive-compulsive natures that come from a mixed place of ownership and desire to control people too much, then people we subjected rage to will have their own voices and their own reactions because human nature does not like tyranny, just as the Founding Fathers escaped from a tyrannical reign to find new purposes to worship in freedom again, their way.

I also learned that being able to hear other people's thoughts, nightmares, and under-the-breath comments is a gift rather than a curse. The Buddha, several Buddhas of the past, were blessed with being able to sense and understand other people's ways of thinking. One prophecy among the Buddhists that I once came across was that of an Arabian prophet who will be able to hear, listen, and understand other people's thoughts and concerns while also performing his tasks as ordained by God, that he, peace be upon him, would turn his body completely around and show respect to the persons speaking to him.

These last few weeks, I gained knowledge that Prophet Jesus, peace be upon him, would occasionally overturn a discussion if it were serious enough just to remind people of their own values, which they supposedly practiced. I think of the scene from the temple in which the worshipers began having greed for worldly things, and Jesus, peace be upon him, reminded them austerely of their real duties.

In Taoism, there is something called the way, and one must persist on that way as if (s)he has never left the way; the more one persists in a simple lifestyle the more the mind becomes aligned to a right path. Sufism teaches something similar, except the way always leads back to God Almighty and that loving fellow human beings in clean and decent ways leads back to Allah's mercy, as many Hafiz and Rumi and Saadi poems go. I am still pondering Sura 54, "The Inevitable Event," which, to me, seems to have some reincarnation elements from ancient ways of thought. Instinctively, I know that Islam, a complete submission to the will of God, is an ancient wisdom, not a new one, and when the Final Prophet came as statesman and logician, he added many more rights than what people were taught to have:

> It is Allah (We) who have created you: why
> will ye not witness the Truth?
> Do ye then see?—
> The Human Seed that ye throw out,—
> Is it ye who created it,
> Or are We the Creators?
> We have decreed Death
> To be the common lot of wrongdoers,
> And We are not to be frustrated
> From changing your
> Forms And creating (you) again
> In Forms that ye know not.

155

And ye certainly know already
The first form of creation:
Why then do ye not
Celebrate His Praises...
See the Water Which ye drink?
Do ye bring it down
In rain from the Cloud,
Or do We?
Were it our Will,
We could make it
Salt and unpalatable;
Then why do ye not
Give thanks?
See ye the Fire
Which ye kindle?
Is it ye who grow
The tree, which feeds
The fire, or do
We Grow it?

I learned these last few weeks that those who try and play God will ultimately get in trouble; they are indeed playing with the fire that God placed in our own hands, which is much stronger than any Promethean discussion from Ayn Rand. Yesterday, I was tidying up a comforter, and I felt strange sparks from my fingertips after having read certain verses in the Quran. Again, I tried to see if the light from an open blind was coming to my fingertips, the right hand, but no light from outside could be seen. I did not understand what was happening, except to guess that we are given a certain amount of light in our hands and hearts with which to heal people and ourselves through the direct light of God. As in many places in the Quran, He calls himself Light. (May Allah forgive me if I am wrong, and I will never wish to be one of the wrongdoers from any path.) Ameen.

Allah is the Gardener who cultivates our thought patterns and understanding of people and this life as we get inklings of the next lives to come. He is the Gardener—as I interpret these lines—who is catalytic and can change the form of anyone or anything should He so desire, Subhanallah. Every Sufi poem, going back to the origin of knowledge, is about taming the ego so that humans can fertilize their own gardens, leading to righteousness for all of us. Since we were born free of original sin, that sin of our bad intentions or deeds can taint us and lead us into destructive paths.

The fruits of our labors come back to us, leading ultimately back to the Gardener, whose plotting no one knows except Him no matter how we think we plan our lives. In that beautiful inauguration, President Biden also noted something on fate, which can trick us into different directions; while we are makers of our destinies in the partial sense, we are not, in the complete and final sense, for the Gardener has placed Himself in charge of our knowledge and our deeds, which return to us in different ways.

By His will, the natural order of the universe retains itself until it doesn't. And we will get judged by throngs at different points of our lives. But people's opinions ultimately do not matter, for each gets his or her chance to redeem himself before God. Ameen.

It used to hurt me—Ms. Nieto's comment during a large English teachers' meeting where she was introducing everyone by their long list of achievements and talents—that *"And this is Kausam. She's just,* well, spiritual." And that was what she said about me. It was as if I were an unimportant contributor to the overall scheme of the school. It was in the beginning of the 2016 Trump year when the excessive self-bragging of each loud person began while putting me down, as many in that department used to do in a public way quite beyond and before my blogging days (an activity for "fun" that a child of mine had once recommended). Now those many humiliating comments and the sense of practiced scorn toward me mean nothing, and as Joe Biden said in the inauguration, "To heal is to remember," which I continue to do through writing and meditation. If God Almighty is our Gardener and the Nourisher of our souls and hands, then only good can come no matter where we live or stand.

Reflections from Al-Ghazali's
The Marvels of the Heart[2]

January 15, 2021

Superstitious people often think that religion is a superstition and that religious people acknowledge that superstitions have no place in religion. Karen Armstrong has noted that "religious people are not the most popular people" while emphasizing the need for religions.

Even Jesus, peace be upon him, was destined to fight demons psychologically, and the Prophet, peace be upon him, had to fight those who continued to threaten him and his peaceful way of bringing Islam to the people. If such blessed ones can fight demons, then what an example for the rest of us. We are able to succeed with God, not without Him, as popular culture presupposes.

One thing both superstitious and religious people might agree on is that while all humans are capable of having bad, demonic sides within, the complete demonization of other entities is nothing less than bigotry leading to the extremism of hatred in the human heart. This is not a time for me to round up all the passages from the Good Books regarding the extremism of hatred for something found in virtually all religious as well as humanistic-atheistic books alike. I once put away a favorite Stephen King book, as rich and successful as he is, for the levels of animosity and hatred that it inspired (it's

---

[2] Al-Ghazali, *The Marvels of the Heart: The Revival of the Religious Sciences*, yranslated from the Arabic by Walter James Skellie (49 Mockingbird Valley Drive, Louisville, Kentucky 40207: Fons Vitae, 2010).

not my place as an average writer to say which of his famous books inspired that much frenzy of hatred in me). So I walked away from it just as I walked away from a certain race-restricting movie I was trying to watch alone after a long day of teaching and grading papers of students whose lives and futures I was very fond of, too fond of, so I had almost forgotten to pray to Allah for gratitude as often as I should have prayed.

I have become good at walking away from people and situations that inspire hatred in me, even in a retaliatory sort of way, and that walking away has been good for me, even being pushed away due to a Pandora's box of resurging hatred of the other that this nation experiences every time a Trumpian character comes around to lead it.

Al-Ghazali al-Tusi was born in Tus, Persia, in the year 1058 and died in 1111. I was most fortunate to borrow this book from a dear cousin of mine as I explored his immense library while taking a getaway from regularly scheduled home duties. I also borrowed some political books about America's liberties, and for me, the two readings were quite related to each other since I tend to be as secular a person as I am a religious one.

Al-Ghazali reminds us that "Satan tempts the heart of those who fear God"—a concept found in most of world literature but especially found in the Quran. I found this precept to be true the more I walked in the path of God, and the more I walked the more I found people trying to tempt me to do things I would never do out of love and respect for Almighty: drinking, sitting idly and gossiping for no reason, spending too much time on the Internet (my own flaw, which I did as I graded or read things), imagining that other people's lifestyles must be more interesting than mine, etc. None of these temptations helped quench my desire for knowledge beyond traditional books and entertainment, which most people seem satisfied by.

Al-Ghazali quotes an Abu Hurayra Hadith that is both funny and thoughtful:

> "The demon of the believer [I assume any
> religion in which God is first] met the demon of

the unbeliever. The demon of the unbeliever was sleek, fat, and well-clothed, while the demon of the believer was emaciated, disheveled, dust-colored, and naked. The unbeliever's demon asked that of the believer, 'What is the matter with you that you are so emaciated?' He replied, 'I am with a man who names the name of God when he eats, and so I remain hungry. [The demon has little influence.] He repeats the name of God when he drinks, so I stay thirsty. He says the name of God when he dresses, and I continue naked; and when he perfumes himself he repeats the name of God and I remain disheveled.'

The other said, 'I dwell with a man who does nothing of all this, so I share with him in his food, his drink, and his clothing.' I would not want any demons to win over my love for God Almighty, if such a spiritual competition is even happening! While most people compete with their sports teams' winning sides, I feel the urge to compete with those who demean the Creator, and show extra respect to our Creator, instead of following whatever demons are thinking about [starving for spiritual nourishment].

What is fascinating about this anecdote is its similarity to the Cherokee version of the two wolves: one wolf goes hungry due to the lack of attention we give it, and the other wolf, to whom one gives one's good deeds, is fed. Thus, we discourage ourselves from doing bad deeds to ourselves and other people. There are other layers of meaning also, but that is not the point of this. I want to understand why people tend to give in to their inner whims, impulses, and demons, which may come from the whims and impulses of hatred and destruction. And I find it remarkable that there are so many people I have met who remain sturdily against the odds of getting inspired by demonic activities that help neither the mind, the heart, the body, the soul, nor fellow beings.

I also observed today that the very last section of the Holy Quran discusses other life-forms besides humans—that God Almighty, in His infinite powers and wisdom, created the djinn, who can be pious and of good character or impious and of bad character and who acts on impulses and fiery delights of chaos on earth.

When I was very young and was being babysat for a few hours, I had a vision at age four that someday, I was going to meet (or see) horrifying, red and multicolored beast-like creatures no matter how much I followed the instructions of my mom and dad and God. The image was very real; it could not think or read like normal humans, but it felt what the human was feeling without any sympathy or empathy. It was bright like fire but not bright like light. Its large head was coming out of an open window with many parts or presences as part of it, and I did not scream once. Still, for a four-year-old, that memory reminded me never to do wicked things to other people on purpose and to never to disobey God on purpose.

Years later, a science-loving aunt with a biology degree would tell me haunting stories about real-life djinn that certain villagers had seen in the mountains near Afghanistan or Sindh. She would say that djinns and demons can be found in every part of the globe just as humans of all races and backgrounds are diverse in getting their glory from Allah Almighty.

The weak Hadith that Al-Ghazali quotes from Al-Darda goes like this:

> God has created the djinn of three sorts. One sort is snakes, scorpions, and creeping insects of the earth. Another is like the wind blowing through the sky. The third sort is subject to reward and punishment. [This makes me think of most public schools that rely too heavily on Skinnerian Behaviorism that does not end up helping the students for life.] God, the Exalted, has also created three kinds of humans. One kind

is like the beasts, as the Exalted said, "They have hearts with which they do not understand, they have eyes with which they do not see, and they have ears with which they do not hear. Those are like livestock; rather, they are more astray" (7:179).

Allah also guides believers to follow productive and decent rather than mischief-making ways in society. As one thoughtful journalist on MSNBC said today (I cannot recall the smart, middling journalist's name right now), "To be a good citizen is hard enough. That is a job in itself, which most people have trouble following."

The Bible also mentions the necessity of using one's eyes, ears, and hearing for doing good activities on earth rather than causing havoc to people unnecessarily.

A nother kind [of human] has bodies that are those of human beings and spirits that are those of demons. [This reminds me of people who demonize others like me due to their own actions being demon-like as projections of their behavioral and thought impulses.] A third sort are those who will be in the shade of God, the Exalted, on the day of Resurrection, the day when there is no shade save Elis shade alone.

This proves useful to me as I seek newer outlets for my creativity so that it is in private for myself and my wish to be better connected to God's mercy rather than man's demonic ways in this world. How few are good citizens who go about their way without disorganizing other people's lives from their organized and barbaric crimes.

Al-Ghazali also asks the harder question: "But how can Satan appear to some men and not to others? If one sees his form, is it his real form, or is it an image in which Satan appears to him? If it is his real form, how is it that he is seen in different forms? This aspect reminds me of what psychopaths are capable of doing—becoming chameleonlike in their behavior patterns with different people. I am only guessing that they are capable of rebelling totally or partially against God Almighty just for fun or out of a DARE contest in the Miltonic style. Just saying no to Satan is as hard as saying what dumb schools try: "Just say no to drugs." And all the wickedness-practicing kids smile at that since they know many young teachers engage in drugs as fervently as they enjoy their cereal in the morning. I wish I didn't know these things, but I choose to use all the faculties that God has gifted me with as He has on those who bury their own gifts. When God's love is one's only drug, amazing sight and hearing can be found within.

Al-Ghazali continues to probe the human mind:

> If Satan is in his real form, how is it that he is seen in different forms? How can he be seen in two places and in two forms at the same time in such a way that two people see him in two different forms? Know that the angel and demon each have two forms, which are their real forms. These are not perceived by natural sight, save only by the illumination of the prophetic office. The Prophet only says Jibril, may the best blessings and peace be upon him, in his true form on two occasions. Once the Prophet asked him to show himself to him in his real form, and Jibril appointed for him a place, Baqi. He appeared to him at Hira and filled the whole horizon from East to West. He saw him again in his true form the night of the Heavenly Journey (al-Miraj) [one of my aunt's given names], at the lote tree of the boundary. [The lote tree has many spiritual and symbolic meanings across eastern and Middle Eastern nations.] But for the most part he saw him in the form of a man. He used to see him in the form of Dihya al-Kalbi, who was a man of a goodly countenance. For the most part he

(the spiritual being: angel or demon) unveils an image of his form to the people of unveiling (ahl al-mukashafa) and possessors of hearts (arbab al-qulub), and thus he appears to one of them while he is awake; this man will see him with his eye and hear his speech with his ear. [Not fun when it happens.] This will take the place of his real form. In like manner he is revealed to a majority of good men during sleep. [Quran, we know, mentions the connection between sleep and death and how Allah is in charge of making us alive again after a restful sleep; I find this fascinating too.] Revelation during waking hours is made only to one who has attained such a high rank that the occupation of his senses with the things of this world does not prevent the revelation which comes in sleep [life story for me since childhood], so he sees while awake what another sees during sleep. (112–13)

This is enough for me to digest right now as I endeavor to understand the surreal things that few like to talk about during normal waking hours. I have also discovered that the few people in this part of the universe who can attest to knowledge gained during sleep are people I relate to much more than people who can talk about the things of this world—the glitz, glamor, and changing styles of celebrities who live or die by suicide or crowds. I do hope that the four-year-old version of me is consistent with the fifty-five-year-old version of me, who has attempted to find my straight path to God even through the perversities of the ways of the world. "This is a Quran in Arabic in which there is no crookedness," says Allah, and that phrase has become more real to me in the conscious hours, when people of all chameleonlike forms take on newer and more scientific shapes and facades.

What I know now after years of suffering for the sake of Allah is that the delusions and illusions come mostly from this world, that reality is in the next worlds, and that God is the only reality (ultimately). And semantics between the two concepts are the moments we are living in the present world. Still, regarding our respect for the diversity of life-forms and life itself, who is anyone to call another's thought process filled with delusions when what we do on a normal basis constitutes our normal attitudes to preserving life and liberty as long as we are good, honest citizens a job in itself that most people cannot do without impulsive behavior?

"Whatever Makes You Happy"
Goes Pop Psychology

January 4, 2021

I am glad to say, as Brother Muhammad Ali once said, that I have very few friends now. It's not that I try to be a loner, cruel, aloof or untrustworthy completely. It's just that now I know that with few friends and few relatives, I have now cultivated a relationship with a small group of people I love and who have my back, so to speak.

There will be no more knives in my back when I am not looking and no more whispering uncouth items in my ear about what I should or shouldn't have done with my life. As seen on January 6, 2021—that raging, maniacal assault on Capitol Hill—democracy itself was tested by those who believe in mob mentality, a lack of refinement in thought, and a war-mongering way of life. It reminded me of people who wanted to escape tyranny from an earthly king to practice their own freedoms, their own religion, and their own way of life—the people who thought them doing whatever makes them happy could not compare to the earlier people who fought their way with hardship and genuine love for God's mercy. The people of January 6, whose cruising manhandlers of political women's papers, their sacred environment, and the trust of their fellow Americans, had no relationship to a justifiable revolution; it was a mini revolution egged on by Mr. Trump that, if left alone, will continue to become larger and larger until the greater pandemic is insurgency worldwide (not COVID-19). And if the reverse were true, if Black and brown people were monstrously climbing up those walls, breaking and entering sacred halls, and ganging up on law and order, they would be shot without due process! *And we all know that.* I have seen and been part of the opposite end as one harassed and assaulted simply for being darker, fatter, different, and, of course, a Muslim American Democrat (not MAD in any form or shape) in a Trump-worshiping state.

Yes, indeed, it is not the way of a democratic, people-loving individual anywhere to act selfishly and mob-assault the sacred symbol of a "freed" people. Similarly, no friend of any friend from past relationships practices any sort of ethics when they stand behind cowards and domestic terrorists, pointing filthy fingers at my religion, my value system, as a mere, poor teacher or my simple way of life. My parents did not flee from a disastrous environment, but they chose to come to Chicago as qualified, educated, and quality people who were quite familiar with democracy in India with Syed Jafar Imam and Grandfather Ahmad Reza Karim working directly (as unprivileged but successful minorities) with law and order, education and teaching, dignity and justice for all, and most of all, equality for all people of all faiths. I am thankful that my America-loving parents did not get to see what happened these few days ago on Capitol Hill. They would not only have been shocked but also emotionally devastated as they had traded a good set of countries for the best country on earth. I am also thankful that my parents did not see all the torment, deceit, and slander that I had to overcome simply by being a Muslim who does not do whatever pleases her, as hypocritical hedonists tend to do while holding up the flag that stands for "In God we trust" yet not standing equally for human beings, made to be flawed and sinful if they do nothing to overcome their own calloused souls.

Imagine if people started doing whatever feels good for the moment. Where would family life go? Where would human bonds and trust go? Where would commitment and one's word of honor go? Would our own word with God disappear? No wonder there are people in certain parts of the globe right now waiting to see when true law and order—with righteousness—come back to American soil so as not to completely destroy the amicability and justice that were written for this nation by destiny. By rational intuition, I am also certain there are even more tyrannical despots in some parts of the world who do not practice their own faiths or ethical systems, ready and waiting to make the next move on American soil. Small acts of terrorism on one soil inevitably lead to larger acts of terrorism on the global soil just as suicides and homicides tend to be copycats of each other in school situations of predatory, low-functioning estates.

But on the fortunate side, when a man and a woman of conscience come into the White House, we might be blessed, particularly if they do not simply hold up a Bible as a stance of superiority but as practicing agents of Jesus's original way of life, which even many Christians do not seem to practice. Peace be upon Jesus, the original one sent by God.

Why should the Divine help us if we cannot even try to help ourselves become better human beings before calling ourselves devotees of any ethical system? Why should we be rewarded for being as malicious to one another as malware in a system made for justice for all? The Quran guides the average, rational thinker with the concept "Allah does not help a people until they strive [key word is *strive*] to help themselves against the worst in themselves (their own egos/nafs)," which seems to mean that we are given the highest faculty above other good animals—free will. Sure, the case might be made that deer and lions have free will also, but not with evolved linguistic capabilities to sort out what is wrong or right, right or left, and extremist or balanced. This does not mean that we should go help ourselves to more of other people's rightly earned things, property, or liberty but to help each other as community members. If the Vikings are a postmodern group, at least they can learn from their own word, *comitatus*, working for the community and not themselves alone. Selfish people lose everything eventually, even when they think they are winning.

Mr. Trump is the perfect example of this: a bright, smart man with many skills in the real world, yet he lost his best people to his own ego, forgetting the God he claims to know. He lost his friends as well as some family members, and with all the intelligence and bravery he has, the cowardice of extreme selfhood became problematic to him. I feel for him because any of us from any community can become as selfish as he regardless of which name we call God, for selfish people might as well say the archaic *God-bye/goodbye* to God if all they care about is worshiping their own might against all odds. If I am wrong in my assessment, I am sure those ego-worshiping thinkers can reread those parts of their own Bible, which still guides people toward becoming less selfish and ego-driven.

It is better to know a few people who believe in everyone's liberty than mobs of people who believe in a few people's liberty. One's religion is not the problem, but one's manners and attitude matter. One's God is not the issue; however, one's ability to help many at one time does matter. One's skin color and weight are not problematic. However, one's soul and heart do matter in the bigger spectrum, for the nation's cause leads to the heart of God's cause. This is the God who made humans gifted, loving, helpful, and sacred. It does not matter by which name we choose to call God as teachers are not meant to be preachers nor citizens politicians.

If we are not careful about everyone's law and order mattering, we also know that history is bound to repeat itself; history teaches us more about our flaws than our successes—that is, if we are meant to be a great nation. If we'd like to be puppets of China and Putin, that is another matter... I would not.

As far as I am concerned, I wish the best for those people who live each day with a whatever-makes-you-happy motto. But that is not me and never was how I lived my life.

Postmodernity itself is a fragmented literary movement, and the age of apathy that might come afterward has most people reeling in the "living in the moment" kind of feeling. Many people who did not completely understand me also thought I lived in this way—love the moment only with no thought for tomorrow. If I ever had such a mood, I surely was on the wrong path, as I see now, because now I see that each tomorrow is filled with how we spent today. How many people have we all met in life who do excellent, happy-making things then regret that particular mood of the moment? Too many. The young woman in England who wanted to live in a desperate moment of running away with a fundamentalist and angry sort, claiming to be a "Muslim," caused only further devastation for herself and her children, whom she claimed to love. Her "cause" as an emotionally immature person was certainly the cause that Allah talks about in the Holy Quran. We humans (and good Muslims who submit fully to our Maker) never choose the path of destruction for others, for only He chooses whom He shall preserve or destroy based on His own mercies.

The pain-pleasure cycle continues in life no matter what we do. If we are aware that pain will happen inevitably at certain points, we can choose to be content that pain is coming soon. When I fell on my face in my front yard—one of my worst accidents after coming from a writing session related to my dissertation and teaching community college—I did not feel pain as much as I should have, based on my extremely bent-up arm, elbow, and shoulder.

I simply saw the blue-purple sky above and had a Van Goh moment, praising the Almighty for the beauty He gave us to appreciate in this world. For whatever reason, that pain melted into a moment of inevitability of accidents, and it did not matter whether I would be alone, living long, or dying. The good neighbors came to my aid and had me taken to the hospital as my family came back from the movies, where I had not chosen to go that evening.

To be serious about life requires thinking. To be compassionate to oneself and fellow beings demands intellectual work after suffering, not only the heart. What is my purpose? Is it to give people pain or pleasure, suffering or comfort, complaints or alleviation of life's problems through various spectrums even if they are in a point of discomfort? After all, it is in discomfort that we grow and learn how to be better versions of ourselves.

Emerson once noted in one of his short essays that what he appreciated most about the Quran was God's advice to stay away from people who "jest about their religion" too much, and it's because these people are more interested in living solely for the pleasure principle rather than accomplishing serious things for themselves. I may not write for some lofty, publishing audience, and as Allah is watching when I appreciate my life through Him, I experience the pleasure principle through the misunderstood angle of contentment. One can be content in life without feeling the need to be screaming with excitement all the time, which is what today's commercials and movies are about: do whatever makes you happy; do whatever floats your boat. Well, doing whatever can cause people to do much harm, to ignore their elders, to neglect their families, and to watch people dying from the inside and do nothing about it. Doing whatever can cause people to make babies without ever intending to care for them.

Doing whatever makes you thrilled can cause people to run off with people while leaving their special family members in the lurch, forgetting all responsibilities for the time being. Doing whatever is a common act by people who follow common principles. How different are we from beasts if we are just focused on whatever makes us happy—floats our boats—while watching other boats sink?

People in big schools and small community colleges talk about team work all the time. It is what makes big speeches happen. "Let's be united," goes the motto as the quiet, creative thinkers on each team are left alone, neglected to the harm of the rest of the team. Sometimes, or too often, those quiet thinkers can offer intuitive knowledge that others may not have thought of; though they may be from different intellectual or emotional backgrounds, their contributions in hospitals, churches, mosques, temple settings, or universities can cause huge and instrumental changes. The African American woman representing Moderna was such an instrumental catalyst who helped with the vaccine for the coronavirus. The quiet, circumspect German couple from Turkey did not live excitedly for every moment, yet they were focused on the personal responsibility of coming up with the cure rather than complaining about problems the majority of "happiness-loving" people complained about. Yet stubborn stereotypes persist about all categories.

From a spiritual point of view, just as the newer Christians were being persecuted for a long time in Rome while Islam was in its infancy, the Quraish and other tribes who were the "superpowers" of the time period were persecuting the Muslim peoples. God revealed in Sura "Romans/Rum" about following through on one's responsibilities to the community's wellbeing while worshiping Him. Of course, the prophecies made in the Quran came true as history showed us what happened to the arrogant ones living for hedonism only:

> The Romans have been defeated. In the low-est/closest land, and they, after their defeat will be victorious. [Indeed, the Romans were victorious, just as Allah said they would be, and those who followed the Roman]... He helps to victory whom He will. He is the Mighty, the Merciful, It is a promise of Allah. Allah fails not His promise, but most of mankind know not, [how many happy-happy people today jest about any lines from the Quran, Muslims as well as non-Muslims, until they become shocked as lightning when truth strikes them?] They know only some appearances of the life of the world, and are heedless of the Hereafter. (Al-Rum 30:2–6)

The point is that we humans are so full of ourselves and our so-called base needs for pleasure all the time that we forget our priorities and are shocked by signals that there are other things in this world—other people, other responsibilities—beside our needs to enjoy gold, swimming, drinking, lusting, eating, vacationing, slandering, etc. All these habits can cause people to have a good time until the good times become the worst times of all, paradoxically. The good becomes the enemy of the great, and the great becomes extinct until posterity...or heaven, for that matter.

From an emotional standpoint, people who are too busy looking for instant gratification through education, their careers, their spouse, their children, or their money are rarely content. And those who are content can handle themselves maturely when the bad times hit them. And bad times will, indeed.

When Objectification
Becomes the Object

November 26, 2020

Every day could be Thanksgiving, but today it was the formal version of Thanksgiving 2020. Still, we look for possibilities and potentialities for the nation as we do for each family. Once we come to terms with our own limitations, great things begin occurring.

This was the hope many had in President Donald J. Trump: to guide the nation back to law and order, a consistency of protocols, and honoring all of America, not just the parts that he knew well.

It was almost like reading of another objectifying hero of oral literature: T. S. Eliot's *The Love Song of J. Alfred Prufrock*, whose hours, minutes, and seconds are consumed with how others view him rather than how he views his own historical works and deeds. It is as if Donald J. Trump is still in the mind-life of his past vision as a leading businessman leading a television show leading thousands of self-helping, successful yet self-consumed businessmen wondering passionately when their next great moment is coming and who it revolves around. "In the room the women come and go, talking of Michelangelo"—this stanza repeats itself at various intervals in the dramatic monologue at a time when Eliot was also preoccupied with the stagnation of the economy, the "wasteland" of morality, and the decadence of people's lifestyles in the late 1920s.

President Trump's beginning in the presidency came off as him being a multifaceted individual leading the way toward bigger and better things (always in comparison to President Obama; a big concern for President Trump was where President Obama was born, apparently, and that he must do much better than the "mere" Black man). A "personal *die mai tornasse al mondo"* suggests a divided personality in a personal war with his own vision for the nation that hadn't come together just yet in the name of "making America great again." Time continued to progress too fast for the visionary filled with many ideas at one time, consumed by the "yellow fog that rubs its back upon the window-panes," as if time itself had to bow down to his powerful image. But time does not back down or rub its hands on anyone. Time races along, and the lone ranger must move forward with time rather than play here and there on green escape lawns, demotivating himself with the conflicted image of what a "true" politician should be and could be after Obama, the Peace Prize-winning president who must be brought down. Today, we have a comparison-driven society in which each person tries to outdo the other, and this problematic obsession with one's accomplishments, fast or slow, brings people greater distress than doing things at one's own pace yet with a knack for timeliness. While each person thinks they have some degree of divided parts of their own natures, projecting them onto others at times or worrying about the least important events, forgetting about the essential needs of the age (not the stage)—a certain inward reflection, even a short series of reflections can assuage the smartest of men to do the unexpected. And I am not talking of ostentatious peace treaties with the Middle East that most of the world knows are only for the few and not the majority as award-winning Netanyahu drones another part of the enemy-labeled city.

Just as Prufrock's love song is solely about him (the ironic title)—desires and anxieties, where he fits in the cosmos of the changing landscape—President Trump's love song for the nation is also on a similar war path, filled with fearful angst and distress, disguised as extreme feistiness and positivity for the present and for the future, and dressed as overconfidence and scornful self-defeatism.

Again and again, we teachers and thinkers have seen this boyhood overconfidence fog up the sharp minds of its personalities, leaving them befuddled about where they fit in the big scheme of things, holding up Bibles (and Qurans that Ayatollah Khomeini types hold up) as the ultimate objectification impulse without ever reading/

practicing a word—all the while as peaceful protesters need much, much more from him than a section of law enforcement that practice brutality before careful observation. A simple moving-forward speech, for example, can bridge the past distresses; a relaxed presence at the table can mend a few minds that have already been made up toward history. Positivity and feistiness must be balanced with a realistic awareness of the inner state of the nation.

Prufrock asks, "Do I dare disturb the universe? In a minute there is time for decisions and revisions which a minute will reverse." He suddenly shifts his focus from a boyhood-centered persona, still not matured into adulthood by his stream-of-consciousness physical pleasures and sorrows with women: *"For I have known them all already, known them all—have known the evenings, mornings, afternoons, I have measured out my life with coffee spoons; I know the voices dying with a dying fall...* And I have known the arms already, known them all—Arms that are braceleted and white and bare...is it perfume from a dress that makes me so digress?" Our president is in a similar position emotionally, it seems: perturbed enough about how others think of him ("They like me"—his favorite saying) and disturbed enough about how much of a difference he is making in comparison to that other guy. We wonder at all, as Prufrock figures, "Why have you known them all...evening, morning, afternoons" (without quality time, commitment, or monogamous dedication). Were you misogynistic in your claw-like attitudes?

This is when anyone with common sense and intellect begins to falter: why compare his energies and productivity to those other family guys—a totally different personality set (in this case, Joe Biden and Barack Obama)—known to attract people through their genuinely smooth and empathic faculties as well as the rational ones, a rare thing nowadays no matter how much an entire public vows adorations and symbolism on their chosen one.

Existing between overconfidence and underconfidence, the imbalanced persons—Prufrock and the former president, not reelected by the public—with all their capabilities and artistic ways of seeing things, end up lingering on time's chariot/limousine too long, wasting the necessary resources and energies needed to accomplish the basic things first before worrying about the luxury items of rebuilding the nation for better and more jobs, personal freedoms, and the right to bear arms (and the women's arms) to protect oneself from overheated audiences expecting more than a giver can give.

Proverbs 27 tells us about the problem with overconfidence in the mind before one acts into confidence: "Don't boast about tomorrow, for you don't know what a day might bring. [Time is of the essence, not our words.]"

Today (when I wrote this last year) patients are lying "etherized upon a table," and they are not objects. Today children are being neglected in schools and homes, and Google-teaching is not enough to stop them from wasting their academic times and refocusing their energies for productive mind management. Children are not numbers. Too many families, Trump supporters as well as Biden supporters, are suffering the loss of jobs, careers, and even food on the table this Thanksgiving 2020 (as our collective vision clears up), and the Prufrocks of the world worry about inconsequential things such as this: "They will say: 'How his hair is growing thin!" My morning coat, my collar mounting firmly to the chin, / my necktie rich and modest, but asserted by a simple pin / they will say, how his arms and legs are thin." Audiences and the American people who are not audiences and patients care more about human suffering and building unity among disunited people than what someone's presence looks like and how many buildings are erected in their name. Nobody cares when one doesn't care—not in any job capacity from bricklayer to the president. Prufrock's distress also occurs in Trump's persona; unfortunately, when he escapes the reality of not wanting to appear before a desperate public, when appearing before people used to consume him, "I have heard the mermaids singing, each to each. / I do not think that they will sing to me." Like Master Hamlet, whom Eliot mentions in the poem, Trump is still indecisive about what to say and how he should think of exiting properly rather than leaving a greater mess in protocol for those who record history. His-story is not always a pretty picture when written by extreme feminists, which I am not.

Certainly, as President Trump's own niece, Mary, has noted, whom he must have disowned by now, one can do amazing things with one's range of emotions even if they are on the shallow levels of soul experience. However, if plugged into the wrong sockets at the wrong historical moment, those emotions turn to dust, as people eventually do, while misusing people who cared for the former president's well-being. Emotional balance is what the fictional Prufrock lacks due to an overactive confidence level fused with hundreds of anxieties. Emotional balance is what our former president lacks, too consumed with objectifying other people on the "enemy lane" who are not truly his enemies; objectifying other people, however, only points back to the instigator of objectification syndrome eventually.

The Price of Everything,
the Value of Nothing

December 2, 2020

Why do people write? For their own reasons, of course. I write to make sense of things in a seemingly nonsensical world where what seems to be true is not often true and what seems to be false may just be true. Oscar Wilde seemed to praise and scoff the cynic simultaneously, as was his custom when he wrote, "Nowadays, people value the price of everything, but the value of nothing."

The pen (*qalam*) that taught the most honorable *ummi*/unlettered prophet can also give the rest of us ordinary minds how to learn, how to think for knowledge, and how to grasp ideas not easily relatable to popular culture. What we learned when we were infants often comes back to us at unusual crisis points in our lives. Thomas Paine's crisis situations gave him newer insight about what he was fighting for—his versions of justice from tyranny and how troubled some of his community members became, seeing him as just another dissident.

My father once shared with me that certain writing styles become me more than other styles. Back then, I didn't know what he was talking about when I wrote my first short essay on what democracy means in concrete and abstract terms. Another uncle in Philadelphia wondered if I should study journalism to discover the world around me and share the relevant findings with fellow thinkers. Mrs. Weimmer liked my poems way back in high school, which I didn't always understand myself; we all change as thinkers and as writers no matter what profession in which we try to immerse ourselves. But now I realize, after all the difficulties life has shared with me, that I may have chosen the wrong profession after all, at least not in the cut-out versions of what teaching has come to mean today.

I did not value the journey of writing for discovery while I was teaching all styles of writing, and maybe it's because the school systems do not encourage teachers to be thinkers as well as deliverers of knowledge (which they now like to call facilitators for its more professional ring). Yet few, we know, practice the facilitation of discourse because this is much harder to do in a real-life setting than giving a bunch of facts to disinterested students. Truly, the circus performance works as a better metaphor for what helicopter administrators expect from average teachers, leading to good grades with mediocre performance (unless students know how to learn and think for themselves).

The price of learning is an exercise in valuing everything: all experience, all people we have had the destiny to learn from, and all things that have come into our vistas. Writing, like learning, is a broader category of experiences, which is why the literature field enables people to branch out and borrow teachings from many areas: philosophy, linguistics, psychology, history, cultural arts, sociology, sciences, and of course, religion. Ibn Rushd, the father of secularism, thought such things as natural in his treatise on contemplation—coherence.

These days, however, we force ourselves to fit learning into categories and boxes so that students do not come away with grasping layers of learning but instead, browse only the titles, summaries, and others' interpretations of what they are said to study. This great disadvantage to keen minds is inhibiting our students from picking up their pens and going from there after what they have read, researched in class, or shared with groups that is different from their own thought processes. This disadvantage in only teaching for narrow expectations has caused our students to falter short of the global knowledge many countries emphasize over specific knowledge, both equally important for growth.

Various attitudes among teachers, as well as with students, create a kind of dissonance as they impart knowledge that is new to students: hatred of other cultures, shocks about historical images, apathy toward parallel universes, and phobias about themselves as teachers and culture historians.

To write along with teaching seems to strengthen the curricular grasp not only for students but for the elders in the room as well. To develop an open mind means to embrace all avenues of learning from distinct fields that one may not be an expert of but a declared researcher. This way, students are making sense of the new concepts piece by piece instead of just taking notes of what a "facilitator" imparts through selected group leaders. The more one learns through the pen or computer, the more those detriments to learning begin disappearing as a disease disappears from one's body: fear; a loathing of wisdom, not just knowledge; angst about "invaders" who may not see themselves that way; and animosity toward other pupils not like themselves.

Discovery of knowledge through daily writing, some research—without worrying about performance (a problem that schools need to deal with)—causes the brain to become liberated from man-made fears and excessive man-made ideologies that may come across as "established" until they are tested with a microscopic lens, revealing they are not always empirical in nature. This is analogous to my young people at home choosing to clean the kitchen through keepsakes and throwaways. In haste, it is easy for young people to say, "This doesn't belong anymore, and this piece does belong." Until that item, which was the most useful in the kitchen, is recalled during breakfast or a soup dinner, people may not see its relevance. This is the same way we treat people and concepts in today's realm of experience: discard people and concepts before understanding what their particular purpose was in the big scheme of things. Similarly, the girls cleaning the kitchen by choice might register the most useful item as part of a "set," and the "lone" dish or unusual museum piece as "offsetting" the set. In writing for discovery, every piece matters, just as every life matters in the classroom, regardless of how they do not match the set.

Each piece of knowledge we gain through study, curiosity, or contemplation does not "kill us" but teaches us, rather, to value beyond ourselves—a value that a throwaway society does not quite understand as still another boss high up in the empirical world discards the out-of-way scientists such as Dr. Fauci—whose advice to the rest of the world is actually valuable.

Just as every essay does not come neatly packaged in a five-paragraph theme with a thesis statement in the perfectly designated place, as most students are taught, wisdom does not come to us in boxed quantities but in quality—not in a semester or overnight but in allowing the brain to allow for understanding through the trials of experiences.

Confronting Our Hypocrisies in an Age of Disappointment

All are not saints that go to church [or mosque, temple, synagogue].

October 13, 2020

On the surface level, it really doesn't matter for some people if we are all hypocrites or not. Not being truthful to oneself can be fun, a character role play for some people—that is, until there are those crises that come out of hypocrisies when all insecurities come tumbling down. "Security is mortal's chief(est) enemy," Shakespeare has one of the witches say. (Apparently, real witches like turbulent, bubbly atmospheres where the pot is boiling with wings of creatures.) The opposite of this is true too: "Insecurity is mortal's chief (est) enemy," as the Shakespeare impersonators of the bard's day had toward him.

Having overconfidence in one's abilities or power can lead one to the worst soul falling, which is heavier on life's path than social-status falling, which can happen anywhere, anytime. I have always known that a middle ground between confidence in one's knowledge base and trust in God's grace creates a dual purpose while leaving one free from the worldly aspiration methods. No one knows how much or how little we know until we need to know how much to know while surviving any inquisition or difficulty.

In Urdu, the word *naseehat* (an etymological cousin of the Arabic equivalent) doesn't have a perfect translation in English. But I will try anyway. *Naseehat* is nagging with unwanted counseling (or self-counseling, as my parents did) in critical overtones that many cannot handle, especially if the advice comes unexpectedly. Rarely are today's school-to-factory-produced children taught how to take good criticism, well-meant or not. *Sohbet*, another Urdu and Persian fusion, is one's ability to learn from all people and all circumstances by a genuine acceptance of others' knowledge base. A combination of *naseehat* (nagging critique) and *sohbet* (acceptance of each person's knowledge base) can be a great method to put aside the socially learned phenomena of Dorian Gray.

Excessive privilege can actually be a hindrance for long-term success because too many privileged people allow themselves to refrain from taking off their Dorian Gray mask while doing a bare-minimum-work (BMW) analysis, studying the soul's mirror for the soul's engine to function smoothly.

As Hafiz, Rumi, and Shakespeare, Ibn Rushd, Thomas Aquinas, Ben Franklin, Sequoyah, Rabia the Sufi, Maimonides, Antonio Machado, Mistral, Spinoza and Gandhi, Leonardo Da Vinci, Emerson, Thoreau, Dr. Martin Luther King, and others did these amazing personages, not only practicing looking into the soul's mirror, but they also took off their stoic social "face" so that they could speak to people as one speaks to his deepest soul or God (as bluntly as the edge of the sharpest heart or sword). The spoilage factor cannot make such souls unfit for themselves or for success. We also cannot teach people anything about life if we are unfit to examine our own selves.

This child-adult, so spoiled by his (or her) family members into thinking that he was their miraculous genius child amid many bright children, could not handle even a short insight into his art collection. Like Dorian Gray, he had trouble looking in the mirror of his own soul, letting the dark clouds on his face cover up the remnants of a sometimes sunlit countenance. (How prescient was Oscar Wilde, recording transformational soul journeys as fiction in all his phases of writing until he found God through his Roman Catholicism by the end of his life.)

When soulful wisdom is taught with reading readiness, it is possible for us not to fall into our successes as we fall into our failures; and failures, many of them, are the root of success, even small successes. When Mr. McCarthy, similar to the larger McCarthy, thought I was not the "ideal" candidate for his big high school production of

Lady Macbeth in the best possible humanistic school, I had to prove him wrong, of course. (In each phase, I had to prove people who were not my family members.)

All the other ten language arts teachers, including my own literary parents, were on my side, but not Mr. McCarthy, who had his favorites in the class—the blonde Rachel, the brunette Kelly, and the other choices—anyone who was not me. "You know more than you should for your age," he said one day, perturbed that I loved Shakespeare so much and knew many of his plays by heart. I was a young threat to his academic well-being. That was going to be the story of my life, which I hadn't known back in high school. Challenges are good for people, and falling from the grace of bad people is just as effective a strategy for success as falling from one's own expectations of our God-given personhood. No one can take from us whatever we have achieved intrinsically or extrinsically, and certainly, no one can take our soul's depth away from us, even in some prison of Guantanamo Bay where the innocent pray their cares away as expert wardens wish they had the peace of mind some of the inmates had. As George Bernard Shaw says, "Beware of the man whose God is in the skies." For some, peace of mind is a small gift if they are already given looks or status; for others, peace is everything, worth more than gold and rubies.

A lovely blue jay flies from one tree to another as I write this, and the thick little squirrel eats of God's sustenance, staring up at the skies as another white-and-gray dove flies into another bush. These are spiritual success stories about creatures of God who do no harm to others but live along their own straight path as each person chooses which path to follow from many paths.

When the parents of the high school community chose me for the role of Lady Macbeth, without my perfectly matching looks or body type, Mr. McCarthy was mad as hell but had to accept the democratic decision from the larger group. That's how egalitarian Manchester Township, Lakehurst, New Jersey, was in the eighties—an ideal school where ideal candidates for many jobs were created due to the competence of their educators and counselors. This Humpty Dumpty was dumped by many people who did not know all the things I was capable of and whose nuts, grass, and leaves only God gave as sustenance when I received little nourishment from those I immediately trusted. This is an ideal way to grow up—trusting some people and mistrusting many other people.

When the performance happened, all he could do was brag about his show above all the other local shows; anything we did as a team was a part of what I had learned—that it takes many kinds to make a successful team work and physical difference has nothing to do with success.

When the kid who liked calling his elders unpleasant names found himself in third place in his well-known projects, he didn't take it very well. He hung his face to the ground as if one failure and criticism can kill his entire spirit. Results of failure do not have to happen in a sulking way—not in theory and not in real life, and a small bit of trust in himself and God would have lifted up his spirits. But again, that is something that anyone who chooses the Dorian Gray route would have trouble accepting because superficial things and quick access to privilege do not make lifelong success. Failures do. Rejections do. Dumping people's qualifications in place of less-enthusiastic or talented people causes others to grow from the soul unit of experiential wisdom, broadening one's creative horizons through spiritual imagination and social discomfort. Then anything can happen, and anyone can grow and blossom once the soul's mirror is examined deeply.

Oppressed or misunderstood people continue growing despite what forceful addicts to popularity show them, as in the case of Dorian Gray, a full hypocrite who had forgotten the precept his author wanted him to know subconsciously. All are not saints that go to church, as the proverb goes. All who plan heavyweight success from the beginning without doing the soul work are not ready for the burden of one's soul success in this world or in the next ones.

The big McCarthy would "hang" people who knew things as witches, weather people, or prognosticating pragmatists. So filled he was with hatred and idiocy despite his intelligence and so filled with provincial thinking about who might and might not be a Communist at heart that he forgot to look deep inside himself for the real witch he was trying to hang all along. If we choose to be realistic, we would not go on witch hunts, blaming every single person for our small failures. I thank Mr. McCarthy, the English teacher who hated me for knowing more than he knew, and I thank the principal who did not see me as "her type of fit," because that meant that I would go beyond a Dorian Gray complex and find my own niche in many fields besides education. We each have something great to contribute in a diverse society no matter where we live, and if this is the America that many founding mothers and fathers envisioned, then we can all do amazing feats without being hypocritical or too idealistic within ourselves. After all, the greatest role model is our own imagination of who we potentially are—even if we are just pests to someone else. I pray for that child who wants to be both artist and scientist, that he lets down his face mask of Dorian Gray and seeks to enlighten his soul by embracing the pain of his small failures so that he can become a success in his own estimation.

Anyone who gave me *naseehat*, nagging criticism, with hate or with love, has become a subconscious part of my own success since the early days of being targeted as "different" in the most democratic high school where a Muslim student, one of three sisters, was selected as being the "high school diplomat representing Christians and Jews." What an irony and treasure that my broad-minded and loving teachers selected me for such a position, going back and forth from Jersey to New York to speak, relating to others' experiences, and sharing our various similar yet different value systems. What kids learn in good high schools certainly can impact their thinking for a long time to come: failures, successes, and the Dorian Gray areas that need reshelling so that we can fill our lack of belief/empty souls, if that's possible, into fulfilled eggs with sunshiny yokes/yolks. Future young politicians, teachers, lawyers, psychologists, and business people can learn so much from studying themselves while studying great books as that of Dorian Gray, and so many future leaders can become more effective leaders if they accept criticism from the smallest people.

Aesop once wrote about the mouse who helped the lion (a gray lizard crawls down a wall near a bush as I finish this piece). The mouse had nothing fancy about his lifestyle, but when the barbed wire was all around the lion of the jungle, only the mouse, with his awareness, could help untie that barbed wire. Today's politicians are so engrossed in their own paths of instant success that they forget to examine how they were in high school and what their patterns of small failures were that the Dorian Grays in them could not accept, embrace, and then let go. Instead, they allowed competition to become their personal barbed wire, stabbing their conscience while filling their egos with fluff. The more critique from others the better we can become; yet society teaches the opposite: critiques are not accepted by "lions" of their jungles. And Dorian Grays focus so much on the extrinsic factors that they soon become unfit to lead their own jungles, thus damaging the rest of the populace or an organization in the jaws of failure. Even Saladin, the gentle king of the Ottomans, allowed and embraced the healing knowledge of the Jewish Maimonides for his son and family, knowing that diversity would enhance his institutional leadership. Today, we all read Maimonides regardless of our religious or secular persuasion.

But choosing two-faced people to help one's cause can only exterminate the cause or hurt one's path, slowing it down, as is happening in politics and educational leadership today. Even the best of parents, being overwhelmed with parenting, forget to tell us that not everyone adheres to the "good faith" rule that we learned in childhood.

Listening to a seemingly small "mouse" can free oneself from the Dorian Gray traps people put themselves in, thereby enhancing one's institution rather than denigrating it. When I would offer critique to the "lioness" from time to time, she had such a hard jaw that any critique was ignored through snobbishness and a hatred of my difference. Yet my intentions were good, stemming from a pure place in my heart; I was seeking betterment for all the teachers instead of the cherished few. Yet being different caused the lioness in the leader's heart to put on more masks on top of masks, letting the Dorian Gray still inside to not even seek out the soul's mirror into enhancement from within. Learning from our failures can indeed lead one into more successes than what we deemed impossible.

Remembering England
in an Age of Trump

September 25, 2020

In another public high school where I tried to fit in as a getaway from its cousin school, a certain tough-talking African American Trump-supporting assistant principal came swaggering in my comfortable tenth-grade classroom with a voice I wish I had cotton balls in my ears for. A cosmopolite in an age of Trump has a hard time fitting in almost anywhere.

"What choo think ya'll be teaching in here?" she demanded. We were reading the polished work of the African American genius playwright Lorraine Hansberry: *A Raisin in the Sun*, in which Beneatha was discovering her African roots. I was teaching the important civil rights play because it was in the curriculum, and the kids were taking an interest in our literary discussion related to family dynamics as well as tracing the characters' heritage. I was letting students do most of the talking, a common habit in most of my classes.

"Ma'am? I am not sure I'm understanding," I said as I tried to take her to my private side of the classroom corner where my desk conferences would happen. "Kids, please continue with the play. You know your parts."

"Look, we don't be needin' no British analogies or whatever un-American connections you try to put in that lesson. As I understand, you be causin' a great deal of mischief to the team." (*How is this director so supportive of Trump?* I wondered privately.) Then, by the tone of her voice, I understood. The Quran reminds the quiet reader "not to bray like an ass" as one's speech patterns matter as much as what one conveys to people.

"I believe each teacher uses his or her repertoire of necessary [global or regional] analogies while teaching in front of apathetic or hard-to-teach learners. While my major was American literature, ma'am, I was raised on British literature."

She did not respond to that as one of her many excuses to come in and shout at teachers at the top of her voice, apparently thinking that shouting was carrying a big stick before one enters a room.

In those three months, it was a joy to see students blooming in a global direction rather than just a provincial one. Even Beneatha in the play was not quite beneath going above and beyond her own realm to image other realms in her past and future that made up the time of her present. While some students engaged in art while reading the play, others had to act out the accents, and still, others were class commentators on meanings beyond the plot. Yes, the students were a joy even though they were shouted at, their desks banged on by angry adults, and they were punished for no big reasons. Leaving was the only choice.

Life is full of ironies, every literature teacher knows. Here, we have a country known for individuality, freedom of speech, and freedom of ethnicity—creed. People had to leave England to be freer here. Yet, irony of ironies, in the Trumpian era, this *cosmopolite* (sounds like my name, Kausam) found herself an unfit American, one who had a hard time taking the perfect position between extreme left and extreme right, both braying at each other and fighting beyond boundaries for the obvious things. True, no one is really a victim in the truest sense. Being true to oneself often requires that few will understand where we're coming from, and I don't mean that in a geographical, nationalistic sense. I mean it in terms of basic, good manners—a very English sense.

In today's era, teaching has become a power play between who speaks the loudest and who can control the minds of students instead of letting them control their own minds through personal discipline management.

Speaking of analogies, with almost every play that I have taught in my lucky twenty-six years of teaching (a small number, considering the years I spent studying literature for fun, not money), unfortunately, I thought of the discursive walks I would take in every trip to England up some green hill onto the brambles near Normanton, Yorkshire, and, of course, toward the treat place on the top of the hill: a cheese pasty shop where I'd have a large English tea with at least two cheese pasties. Units of study are like this: discursive and sometimes imperfectly rambling with small enough analogies to people, places, and things that students can understand how human beings connect with each other despite nationalities and regionalism. Not every work of literature has to stick exactly with that work of literature. "What the Dickens?" we might say. And Dickens's own *Great Expectations* with Pip's misfortunes can just as well be connected to Beneatha's idealistic temperament as much as any other reading analogy that one remembers quickly from the traveled brain.

Today's students need connections from other people and places so that they can broaden the scope of their learning rather than see things from one people's ways.

And down five miles I would walk back home to Virginia House, where my sweetest mother-in-law was waiting for me like any good mother would. It did not matter to me that other people didn't wait for me to come back as they kept busy with their television programs, talks with their friendly neighbor, or most recent football (soccer) match. My mom-in-law thought I was a pretty weird Paki-American anyway, and though I was different from the Indo-British in some ways, we two hit it off pretty well even throughout our small differences.

She was humble and caring, passionate about her children, and devoted to God. She'd wear a tranquil blue sari with the shawl around her shoulders unless she did her prayers—a commonality we shared besides our love of the English countryside and English manners. Live and let live. Be who you are and enjoy one another's personal space.

Speaking of manners, as most English novels have a section on manners and personal conduct, our neighbor Ralph (no one knew exactly what he did for a living), on the surface, was an artist, an engraver, a chef, a jump-across-the-fence-holding-tea-trays, a traveler, a poet, a designer, and a homemaker (some said he was a British agent); but he had the best and kindliest of manners. Around age eighty-five, Ralph was the fittest of fittest, not just in brawn but in brains and good humor. Anyone who could become the chummy-chum-chum of my Dr. Papa, Dr. Salam, my father-in-law, had to be the friendliest man in the world. What they talked about for hours and hours, I have no idea! But Dr. Salam—in his Bihari Scottish checkered lungi with beige or white kurta and cigar with tons of sweets beside his straw floor mat (a preference for his back problems)—and Ralph—in his red wool sweater and dark pantaloons, sitting like Mr. Darcy in the side lounge chaise, crossing his legs, and having fruitcakes and tea—got along so perfectly that sometimes even language was unnecessary between the two chums.

I felt the same way about visiting the historic site of Wordsworth and Coleridge's walking tours: an area in Cockermouth Mountain where my husband and I celebrated our first honeymoon in a small village where they were known for making fresh pastries and hot English tea. We even took my mom there one year as a sort of secular pilgrimage to my best place of good manners. My mom, of course, for the umpteenth time, would mention watching Princess Diana's wedding live, and we'd talk about the details—her from New Jersey and me in Texas, raising my children and going to college (again).

From the local fisheries to the fish-and-chips shops to the local tandoor takeout shops to the corner candy store to the small grocery shops—every single person would not only mind his or her manners but speak with calmness, consideration, and humor, never on the back of someone's honor. That's what I recalled about the English temperament during all those tough teaching moments when pleasing the adults became irrelevant to me as I was making the students' knowledge base grow.

I don't know whether England's clime is still as green and amicable as my seven years of visits there (one reason I was excited that marriage with my husband would ensure our many travels there together). One year, my brother-in-law Anjum's two best friends (one was named Julie, of course, a name I can never go wrong with apparently) felt free to visit us two in Florida, of all places. Our kids were small enough to fit in baby carriages and big enough to barely walk. We chose baby carriages, of course, for this trip was for adults.

Flow selfish we were in younger days, as I'm sure one of my children will chide me. Not only did we live amicably well and in a down-to-earth manner—considering it was too close for comfort with our distinct lifestyles, the six of us adults cramped in a chintzy Floridian hut—but we went out of one another's way to cook surprising things or buy interesting meals for one another.

Unexpectedly memorable trips with family come back in the memory to amaze us with how close we can choose to become with family members who live far from us.

Making Sense Out of Nonsense
Too Much Formulaic
Writing in Schools?

There are always those people in any given class who do not make sense in their writing or speaking. We have all been there, so to speak. Still, it is our duty to preserve what their meanings are while guiding them to make meanings out of their own thoughts. Teaching can be like the work of an anthropologist without apologies for dissecting the fossils out of ancient artifacts found in students' pictorial memories. It also doesn't help when we teachers have to figure out their symbols and childhood fossils left inside their brains from their handwritings and suddenly shifting constructs. This does not mean that every child deserves a perfect grade just for writing or doing an assignment. However, it is the duty of every teacher to decipher the meanings even when meanings are carelessly made on paper.

These are the students who had been so used to violence in their lives that the ongoing trauma of living in and through violence made their writing foggy, unclear, and often puzzling to read. As a teacher, I had to retrieve the sensible parts from the muddled sections to understand such student's written codes. Instead of asking them instantly to revise works, I would have writing conferences about their versions of what the present communications were about.

Montaigne, the originator of the contemporary essay form, would first reaffirm his Christian faith by communicating with the unknowable God. The French phrase "Que sais-je?" (What do I know?) became his personal writing motto as he worked through his problems through writing as a discovery more than a profession of what one knows, as most people write today. Discovery writing allows students to understand where they are coming from, not necessarily where they are going. This relates to children who have been traumatized in divisive families or work-related abuses that their families have undergone—common problems today.

The phrase "*Que sais-je*" gives the writer, young or old, a sense of newness and relativity of experience rather than dealing with absolutes. The Quran also talks about taking the middle path, as do ancient Buddhist writings in figuring things out for oneself between what seems wrong, right, peaceful, violent, etc. The middle path and "*Que sais-je*" allow writers to keep an open mind while dealing with their many traumas. Today, there is hardly anyone out there who hasn't been part of some big trauma or experienced it vicariously through close observations of others, well intentioned or otherwise.

One of the reasons that I chose teaching for my original profession way back just before marriage (over journalism and psychology—two areas in which teachers had given me awards) was to allow the empathy inside me to guide fellow thinkers, as I would call students, into deciphering their own codes of self-understanding. When we understand all that we are capable of, then can we simultaneously understand what other fellow thinkers are capable of and have lived through directly or vicariously.

America has two choices to make if she wants less violence in her traumatized young students, and other countries may follow if we were to treat all students and teachers equitably: (a) Stop making violence an entertainment for a hangry audience, because I have witnessed young people's drawings with their writings—injuring others, their siblings or parents, structures, and animals. I have also witnessed in the state of Texas (after leaving a certain job due to their violence toward me for no obvious reasons) countless small dead animals along the roadsides near their schools—dogs, cats, raccoons, skunks, deer, reindeer parts, big birds, etc. Because I am a Muslim and love creatures and all beings (except for the violent), it was devastating to see such violence of body parts splattered on the roads, parks, streets, etc. during the four violent Trump years, coincidentally. And (b) allow fully educated teachers to encourage students to explore their own thinking patterns as much as they love teaching the "formulaic writing styles" that most good college professors do not say prepare students for academic or creative work later on.

If American students are not just going to compete with other European nations on the larger spectrum of education, violence as entertainment needs to be minimized with our increasing levels of sociopathy and psychopathy in violence-reared adults who also have trouble with family life. If we borrowed Montaigne's concept of *essayer* and try to think things out as a learning process (rather than as a product), we will ask, "What do I really know?" And how accurate is what I know compared to my previous knowledge base a few years ago? Even the most blind-sighted students would be able to incorporate all the God-given faculties of sensing, perceiving, thinking, and feeling and at least twenty other senses that today's schools do not focus on for the holistic well-being of their traumatized students. This might even assist some of the violent police officers going into a warzone, not being liked as a profession since the Black Lives Matter movement and not being trusted as a group due to common trends in not following through with due process before shooting the "messengers."

However, if we do not mind violent children in society who mimic the patterns of more violent teachers and parents, then all we have to do is train them to sit in front of the icy television, let their hearts bleed until they are sucked dry, and practice the killings or beatings on their siblings and family members then put that comedy on another violent children's shows. This way, America would only harm herself while other nations continue to practice some degree of family harmony even in poverty's sensibility.

Overconsumption of the World Can Cause...

September 22, 2020

There is an old French story called *La Plage* by Alain Robbe-Grillet, in which three children are touring a beach in between waiting for when the bell might ring. It seems apparent, from my reading, that the children were not happy, nestled within the walls of an institution, and neither was I excited to be nestled within the walls of any microscopic institution that only saw itself as a mark of light amid the world's daily horrors, found in textbooks and the nightly news. The children in this story are parallel to nature—enjoying the world's beauty but not consumed by it and learning and leaning on God-given nature but not pantheistic nor contorted by trying to become what they are not:

> *Ils sont blonds, Presque de la meme couleur qu le sable: la peau un peu plus foncee; les cheveux un peu plus clairs. Ils sont habilles tous les trois de la meme facon, culotte courte et cemisette, l'une et l'autre en grosse toile de'un bleu delave. Ils marchent cote a cote, se tenant par la main, en ligne droite, parallelement a la mer et parallelement a la falaise, Presque a egale distance de deux, un peu plus pres de l'eau pourtant, he soldi, au zenith, ne laisse pas d'ombre a leur pied.*

It seems that the three children in this story not only find parallels in their journey, but they also walk parallel in a straight line near enough to the water. In moving forward in a straight line, we see them deeply absorbed in what they are doing in their journey but not inclined to look back at anything else. The seabirds in this story are also parallel to the children and are as pure in spirt as the children are, doing what they are meant to do. Only the interruption of "*Voila la cloche*" as the smaller boy notices disturbs them from time to time.

As the birds fly up, following their own bell for flight, the children, "*laissent derriere eux de profondes emprein-tes*" (leaving deep footprints behind them), are still holding hands and being parallel to the shore and the beach. This profound story symbolizes a rich aloofness with the world but a following of the bell of one's conscience—in the John Donne kind of way—more than any institutional bell, as we teachers know that the school bell does not organize one's life but that one's life's organization comes from a Higher Bell of one's soul-conscience as we find synchronicity and parallelism from both logical and intuitive ways to find ourselves, doing what works best for us.

Teaching was the same way for me: I did not seek the information of teaching from educational sources or expert opinions to know what each student needed to learn in finding his or her own bell of conscience while finding the most suitable fit for a lifetime career, profession, or creative passion. As long as we are not too much into the world, as Wordsworth warned us in his sonnets, we will inevitably carve our destiny with the help of God. Institutions may go wrong. People may go astray if they are not taught to work through the bells of their conscience. Churches, mosques, synagogues, and temples may go wrong if they invest too much time in things rather than people—a common reason why many leave organized religions and chaotically organized schools.

Yet when one finds oneself on an open space somewhere—whether the open space of a house, beach, imagination, or a campsite near mountains, what one can do is monumental. For some, that bell of conscience can go off without the desire for God. For others like me, fie is my first love in the universe, leading me to understanding my family as well as global family: "And pray in the small watches of the morning... O my Lord! Let my entry be by the gate of truth and honor and grant me from thy presence and authority to aid me" (Sura 17:76–83). Once we have our selected open spaces, without the clichés of trite songs of popular culture, the human imagination is boundless, and I suspect that our spiritual growth comes as an outlet from the human imagination.

Outside, there are crimson bluebells growing right outside my writing window. Swift breezes blow the colorful new buds in all directions, in sync with the world of the imagination. Tall white flowers dance in the distance, and I don't need to go and grab all the beautiful things I see, as worldly people tend to do. Seeing these glories of God is quite enough for me to keep growing inwardly, which no institution can teach.

Carbohydrates and Kind Words

September 23, 2020

I have two addictions: carbohydrates and kind words. Most addictions stem from somewhere in childhood, I assume. What some sense is lacking, others might sense as excess. I was always spoiled in love and comfort; I had no need for love or comfort from any other source than from my family. Maybe this was evident when I met people in college for the first time—college friends who felt the need for "something" out of sheer boredom, frustration, anxiety, or lack. Too many college friends felt the need to "become" or "pose" as someone other than who they were. I could see through them, but sometimes, they had trouble seeing through themselves. That is why it was easy for most people from any of our college friends to become "sell-outs" and temporarily join forces with what they knew was bad for them or unhealthy for their spiritual growth or emotional well-being.

I had to preserve as much of my emotional well-being for posterity. This much I knew. With some optimism and blessings, that preservation may have been good for my adult family in the long run. Self-preservation is a hard thing to do—to treat oneself like a museum piece, priceless as a painting—not for the sake of being stuck-up but for the sake of God, for He was always whom I belonged to. I would be saddened for people who did not treat themselves very kindly, as if they were a piece of trash or a temporary carbohydrate in other people's lives. People who often feel trashy about themselves give themselves to trashy substances or trashy-behaving people. This was another reason a healthy detachment, even from my friends, was a good thing for me, which I gained by intuitive knowledge and much reading.

While I did not mind going to occasional clubs in college, the "square" on certain Saturdays, or even the occasional college party, I would make sure that no close-up dancing would happen to me, not by mistake, not by choice, and definitely not by drinking liquor. The dearest friend in college was a Christian Iranian friend, Dini (her name means spirituality), who had stopped me the second I tried a bunch of drinks for the first time in my life. The brown bottle looked just like the rust bottle, which looked just like the green bottle, and if I had imagined what piss would taste like, that's how all of these bottles' contents tasted. I didn't understand that something that gives people such bad breath, stomach cramps, and short-time highs could ever be so popular.

But then what is popular is not always right, and what is right is rarely popular. My true friend Dini simply said, "No, Kausam! That is not you. That is not the girl who prays at night, prays in the morning, and believes in Allah and her religion! Stop it this second" (as if she were my mom and seven years older than me, in her sophisticated tight jeans and pretty sweater, with long hair blacker than shiny black).

We went to our dorm room, and I wondered what it was that made me do such a thing perpendicular to my character. It was upsetting for me that my college buddies had chosen to drink excessively that day and were dancing lewdly. Instead of helping the helpless, who were clearly not proud (later on) of their sleazy behavior, I helped myself into acting just as helpless—not a normal characteristic I knew I had. After washing up and taking the coffee that Dini made for me, saying my prayers, and letting her be the best friend anyone could be to anyone, I called my dad.

He was the kind of father anyone would dream of: kind but tough in giving advice, tough-loving but genteel, and gentle without being pedantic.

"Akka, I have to tell you something. I tried alcohol, too much of it for the first time, and I feel sick and not proud of myself. My friend Dini helped me get rid of that copying that I was trying to do." There was a pause. We always shared our thoughts openly, but there was a pause.

"Beta, you made your choice at a certain point. You've already studied why liquor is harmful for you. You already know your own spiritual consequences. What would that kind of sin do to a body and a mind?"

I paused this time. I had to think it over. There was a reason that I shared this with him after my shower, my ablution, my prayer for gratitude and shame, and my gratitude for my friend—a better Muslim than the Muslims who were supposedly my friends, inspiring me to do things harmful for me.

"Well, sin makes people go numb. It makes people not have any feelings left any more, maybe not a heart for Allah anymore."

"And maybe we justify what we do that's harmful to us by joking about it or feeling proud of ourselves for pretending to be higher than Allah." He added something to that effect. I never forgot that conversation nor my Christian Iranian friend Dini even when she married that guy later on, even when we lost touch, and even when she came to my wedding but did not invite me to hers. Some friendships we remember for a lifetime, more than the empty carbohydrates we take to harm ourselves.

Carbohydrates are my only adult addiction. I know that people I have met are addicted to more harmful things in today's schools and society: drugs, liquor, out-of-wedlock fornication, lust, avarice, envy, cheap lifestyles, hitting people, honking their big cars at small horns, beating people in their friend or family community, competing with each other for stupid things, pornography, trashy costumes while trying to gain respect, etc.

Life is too short for following model people's dieting fads, but I do take care of myself in many other dimensions for my sake and for the sake of God. After all, He is my judge as I leave this world—a place filled with addictive lifestyles.

Having become a better judge of character and lifestyles over the years, my other addiction is kind words from genuine people, just as genuine people are rare in today's addictive, semiglittering lifestyle, which I do not enjoy one bit out of choice and free will. Kind words are disappearing from this culture. The phrases "I'll kill you," "Killer type," or even "Get out" are supposed to be average phrases for average people just as violence has increased exponentially in the movies and in real life. Meanwhile, kind actions and words are few and far between. It is easy to become a common Joe and follow along with the drinking crowd-pleasers that follow along blindly until they don't even know which sins harm them continuously. Detachment was always my panacea to gathering excess sins like excess calories.

And through creative detachment, we can pick and choose which small bad things are not as harmful in the big spectrum of life. When I look back at parenting styles, I notice that the fewer the rules there were to follow in our house, the more people tended to follow those rules. We would voluntarily do dishes, tidy up the kitchen, or help with the laundry not because some refrigerator sign said that all duties should be shared equally but because the adults were doing just as many menial chores as the children. A true sense of spiritual equality was felt in our house on 2424 Steiner Road. And when my college or high school friends would visit, they automatically took their shoes off in prayer areas and automatically called my father Akka as if he were also their dad. And my mom never tried to please the kids with extra compliments or superficial catering but treated each of my friends as an extension of her family.

Parents are truly our first teachers, and what teachers do later on can only help us grow emotionally or solidify our anxious behaviors due to their own behavior patterns, carelessly thrown onto us. The kindest words I ever received from my son were "You really are like Akka in so many ways," and the phrase had nothing to do with my looks, losing weight, whatever I had thought I had achieved in life, my dress, or my lack of worldly sense. All that Akka and Ammi kept teaching generously, despite my readiness or not, kept me going in the hardest times when their love continued on in me despite them having gone to another realm. As my cousin Suboohi says, "That parental love that sheltered us in every storm is still sheltering us in unexpected times today."

On Cowboys

1998

Since then, I belong to One very special entity (and no, He is not an imaginary being): the most special of any presence I have ever met. In times of grief and times of joy, in times of uncertainty and times of ecstasy, *in each moment, my Maker gives me hope that is nothing like I have seen or felt in the world.* To Allah. Ameen. We grow and change due to learning the life that He freely gives. And curiosity with joy in learning is the Muslim's best gift.

I also had never experienced some worldly mobs hating on me when I wrote this poem on a road trip. I guess how we express ourselves is related to how we feel and think in a given time period.

> Every second of the search is an encounter
> with God. (Paulo Coelho)

The issue of belonging is (was) a dear one for me.
At times, the cost of thinking has risen
As the prairie meets the hill,
Nothing to be seen for miles but for the long Texas cowboy
Taming his changing wilderness, roaming with his herd under-
    neath the cloudy blues.
The peaceful landscape scene was once a reverie for me as I'd
    often listen to cowboy poems and songs. I knew no cow-
    boys or their cowgirl mates in all the places I used to live.
    My comrades were preppy young things, fashionistas or
    tomboys in tight city jeans while I wore long combs in
    overall pockets.

Who knows if the face behind the cowboy's hat is brawny
    from too much sun of middling rage, Drifting along his
    longhorns,
Or that his ancestors were the reds of the brave, native earth,
Or perhaps the tribal forefathers figured to leave the Mongolian
    strait
To weather prairie ice in the newest world.
Or the true cousins may be the wild vaqueros of pampas,
Taming their metallic creatures, riding the night with pride.
Or even more daring might be the cousin nomads
Of ancient deserts on silver stallions
When the Arab was just a roaming Berber along the Barbary
    Coast.
Then again I saw the Texan cowboy,
No east-west myth here: The face seems real,
The body, tough—no cartoon cactus near a country hick,
Driving to San Antonio along rows of sky-blue bonnets
Move the truest poets of the land, still needing taming,
Strumming their rhythmic stride
To the tune of Southern wind and rain.
Amen.

Part of a Recorded Dream while Being Pregnant with My Third Blessed Child

July 27, 2001

This dream, which came as a warning, had a profound impact on my life. Its reality had a profound impact on all of our lives.

The person who understood that Allah gives us such dreams as warnings on how to manage lives while keeping all life sacred was my father, of course. He listened to my sweating face and disheveled appearance after I narrated the longer version of this dream to him in my purple journal, which had (later) gone to New York and come back years later with a scholarly Jewish student who volunteered to type some of my journal entries when the back was not working properly.

In the dream, a voice kept saying, "You have to choose between peace and war. All people must choose between eternal peace and eternal war." And many cell phones were going off at the same time with confusion as a backdrop to the extreme violence that was happening all around. Feeling ashamed that I dreamt such a horrific dream, I did not share the entirety of the significant dream with most people I knew at that time, and as we are asked by our parents to pray for people who were suffering, I did just that: prayed incessantly for the ones who were especially affected by the tragedies of the events that the dream foreshadowed.

It seemed that we were all made to be part of those who would choose between eternal peace and eternal war. All people and all nations had to make the toughest decision of all time. More than three-fourths of the people in the dream chose war. War became a way of life, and self-defense after that.

Four people in a gray van sat, amazed at the decision-making process, recording notes through videos, phones, and notepads. War was in human hands again as it was in Bosnia years before.

A man drove the van that I was placed in and asked me permission to park the van at his chosen destination. The roads were not straight. Crooked patterns of hilly places and stones were on the roads. Not one of us in the van told the other what our decision was going to be: peace or war. In my heart, I knew peace would be my way no matter what happened. The martyrs wanted peace also and to be near their loved ones.

There was a permanent war zone for many since this moment, even more than history's moments. Earth's loose things and creatures kept flying in the atmosphere as though anything precious and human life can seem like debris from a distance. The two women in the van had become friends or allies. I could not tell which. Many women were against men who acted as perpetrators of this horrific act. They were womanizing and drunken. The women held hands like little sisters crossing the road to school.

Everyone in the van except me and a few others had chosen war most readily. Was I one of the people flying off like debris, or was it a sister who loved everyone around her in that place of work where many of our families had worked at some point in their lives? It could have been any of our lives. That was the point for feeling how they were treated like debris.

Some of us tried to find a way out, holding on to railings, pipes, pieces of man-made materials, anything. There were too many cliffs and hills to reach the other side, wherever that was, and we kept slipping, falling off the slimy path. A lady police officer's voice screamed out of emergency for all, "Get off our side, or else we'll shoot." Some ended up at the base of the hill where a dirty swamp was. A stranger came walking and talking on a cell phone, arguing with somebody about the logistics—about peace being the only choice, but he was not logical. Another talked on another cell phone from another side.

I tried to listen. The stranger ignored me when I called out shouting to him, "Stop!"

He pointed a finger at me and many like me. He said I would be treated as one of those criminals who could leave a mark on the city. "Why?" I asked? No answer. I said, "You're getting people mixed up in your anger and grief."

"Leave," he said.

"There's a second attack coming fast," said another angry person. Another group would take credit quietly. "Powerhouse," he said, "someone will destroy a powerhouse."

We, on the other side of these attacks, didn't want people to keep attacking innocents, not even one another. Smoke kept coming from the skies as if to remind humans what humans are capable of, not God. Screams upon screams kept coming from the innocents trapped inside. They were people devoted to their loved ones and in the wrong place at the wrong time. They were martyrs who shall be out of this world.

Then came the rescue.

Some were rescued by good officers who gave their hearts, minds, and impulses to the people. Someone fretted alone on the ground after a cold, cold rain.

And blood-close bodies still lay on the ground. Miracles for some were bound to happen. Death's angel, unseen, presided nearby, telling us humans, "Death is kind. Death cannot harm if we believe in God and if we trust in our fate."

In another city not too far, someone hears forever an innocent
    cry,
Feeling the breath of a stranger-friend in the distance.
His prayer blended in song and was heard throughout the same
    blue sky
That carried so many.
Above, there was a clearing.
Clouds moved slowly.
In fives the geese flew high.
After pain, a large suffering relief came for some

207

In the form of a high wind-dust that swept all bodies from the
    ground
And takes the souls away to where they belong in the afterlife.
"Will you choose peace or war?" The echoes were heard.
Observers of surprise attacks were left standing.
There's one in a faceless crowd where children shouted and new-
    borns smiled,
All in a world of thunderclaps and waving winds in a darkening
    sky.
Silent clocks stirred, still resounding,
Where each hand turned its own any which way as functions in
    the body turned
When humans dance, when they lose their way, or when they
    sway
To another turn. Despite time's ticking and loss of pride,
Despite the stench of tombs, which made my human hands
    destroyed,
Some senses boast of winning certain hearts.
Some are traitors to their own cause
As ones stood fighting to the last for this life given us by God
Sober death, somber burial. Do we feel alone?
Survivors bless or curse from their breath.
Some mutter that they were not burned just yet in this war,
    which hasn't been named just yet
Others say, "Hasn't war been the name disguised for slaughter-
    ing those cast aside, of tortured souls and beaten minds?"
Which types of personalities are bent on committing such acts,
    thinking they're heroic for their own bloodlust? Some
    intimidation coming from a beaten man?
Still, the echoes abide: "Do you choose peace or war?"
Peace, I choose, still peace—for those who are still alive
Before we go to our origins.

There were other pages related to this dream-nightmare, but I
cannot find them now. Someday I will learn more from all the warnings that came from somewhere other than myself.

My chest hurt for many occasions after this dream. When the reality of this terrifying dream occurred, I was teaching a Spanish class for which I had prepared a creative verbs lesson that I automatically pushed aside once I knew the tragedy that had occurred. I had a creative planned for them.

When I found out what actually happened, I turned on the classroom television, which I had intuitively set for that week, and let the students watch the news coverage that pertained to all of our lives. My role suddenly changed from teacher to counselor, from counselor to parent, from parent to friend, and to fellow American. I asked my precious students to write anything they needed to write in their Spanish language journals. It did not matter which language they chose to use as their language of relief. We had prayer moments for those wishing and needing to pray their way. And we had moments of silence for those needing to be quiet and not talk at all.

The entire culture of our school building changed. My community college job was still the same. Most of my colleagues at the time were still my colleagues, and while my students treated me the same as always—affectionately, kindly, thoughtfully, introspectively, and obediently—a few adults changed their attitudes toward me. One significant adult even asked the entire audience in the most surprising way a few months later, "So which of our teachers are actually Muslim?" And to our surprise at the question more than the answers, two of us raised our hands like little children: me and an Egyptian teacher (sister) who wore the full hijab.

A year later, I would have special permission to have a guest speaker from the parent community to give a small talk about how most Muslims really lived: not as terrorists but as peacemakers. He was my family friend, a future Trump-supporting Muslim-American (ironically) who was consistently more patriotic than I was: Brother Aejaz. I was grateful to the fair-minded leader at the time for allowing me to invite this speaker who could be more clinical and factual about Islamic lifestyles than I could be. I respected the leader's ability to see all sides of an issue even if she did not agree with certain theological positions slightly different from hers: the way America can be if we truly practice our democracy. At this point, the school served as a microcosm of the democratic vision that many of the Founding Fathers had. Of the teachers who listened the most open-mindedly to the short lecture was the mathematics department and the social studies department. But this is only my elephant memory; I could be wrong.

Nevertheless, 9-11 was the nightmare of all nightmares for me, worse than the serpent nightmare, worse than the Bosnian genocide nightmare, and worse than other personal nightmares; its impact left no one out in this country and the globe, as we all know. It left me feeling burdened and helpless, victimized for the victims as though my being American and a Muslim simultaneously was going to be the hardest role to reconcile with my spiritual emotions and intellect. I could not believe in my heart of hearts that people who truly loved Allah would be perpetrators of this terror. Prayer became a greater part of my life: consistent prayers for everyone beyond security.

Those who lose faith in their various religions due to humans' cruelties blame the god they do not want to know.

Those who love God Almighty with all of our hearts, souls, and minds know that man does cruel deeds to fellow humans and then blames God—the Glorious One who has already given us two highways to choose (between wrong conduct and right conduct) in the treatment of fellow humans and global brothers and sisters—for his indecencies.

Having the trait of foreshadowing or inklings of some futuristic events is not something I asked Allah for in my life. It is not how I wish to be defined. It simply is a part of me, and I have been able to save my life and others' lives by this ability that Allah has given me. I know there are many souls who have similar abilities, and some use their traits wisely while others do not.

In teaching people to find their career paths, this trait of predicting certain aspects of what can happen has helped many students along the way. I have also been able to guide my own children when they ask me for my input; otherwise, I do not interfere in people's plans for their lives, especially if they ask God Almighty to help them. In recent years, I have survived many emotional storms based on this trait that Allah has given me. Ameen.

When we know ourselves very well, we also learn various aspects about fellow human beings and their personalities—as if we were all meant to be part and parcel of ourselves—something Tennyson, Keats, Blake, Hafiz, Rumi, and Saadi knew about very well including how much Tennyson's society scorned him until he became confident about who he was and why God Almighty gave him his varied abilities, which we can all cultivate should we choose peace instead of war inside ourselves.

As I remember, the poet Blake did not once fight with anyone after one insignificant fight in his locale. He lived a life of righteousness with one wife and a true calling: the arts magnified by the spirit of God. When we choose peace over war, no matter what is occurring on the outside of us, inevitably peace settles inside, and there is no greater achievement than peace: an acceptance of how things are with full trust in God. Amen.

We can try to have war on drugs, war on terrorists, war on haters, war on peacekeepers, war on family members, war on fat people, war on thin people, war on anyone who looks different from us, or war on anyone who thinks or prays differently from us. Have we yet solved these wars? Or are they on the rise?

Ultimately (in my spiritual experience), God is in charge of us if we fully submit ourselves to His will alone. (Thy will be done.) If He wants death for me, I accept death. If he wants rebirth for me, I accept rebirth. If he wants success for me or failure, I accept either one. If He inclines me to defend myself and others without exceeding rational limits, I accept the challenge. (Thy will be done.) But holy God (Allah) has never asked any submitter to harm or hurt people or retaliate as Macbeths of the world, never to destroy as terrorists of the world.

And the merciful God that I know and have known has never taken me to a position of eternal war on anyone, for I want to be from merciful God Almighty of no earthly countenance, whose spirit is available to all of us at any time we ask, and not from Satan do I wish to be connected. No, not to that devious, rebel from, misguiding those meeker than him, scorning anyone, and cursing anything that goes for God and for goodness.

Even in joy, there is moderation. If I enjoy talking to a rebel being who makes war on anything he sees as distinct to my friends or my children, that is not all I shall do. If I enjoy traveling with my husband, I shall not avoid prayer or submission timings.

If I enjoy a teaching job in some respectable place where everyone is regarded as an equal human being of equal yet diverse purpose—that is, not expecting everyone to be the same personality: extroverted, loud—holding an imaginary rod with which to beat knowledge on kids' heads. For everything, there is moderation with a purpose (even lecturing, which I hope we are not doing 95 percent of the time because I would fall asleep at droning voices). And having joys/excitements on a job without setting moral limitations is a transgression that can turn into time-wasting desires that can turn into aggressions that can turn into nightmares, as I would advise certain young teenagers who would ask my advice about how far they should go in certain work or life relationships for which highly hormonal teens are known. "Would you want abortions?" I would ask. Then you'd know the answer. Ask your higher self since you asked. The girls who asked such personal questions after their writing portfolios often did not get the answer for which they were waiting, but they did receive the rational answer that may help them avoid a disaster in their lives on a pragmatic level. However, we did not talk religion in a secularist school unless the students wanted to share their spiritual paths as excerpts of their literary experience in their writing portfolios.

"Life is sacred" is a theme found in many literary works. Why do we in society insist on having young people read things in which life is *not* portrayed to be sacred? What do our students gain or lose from hedonistic works except to submit to one's desires or emotions at all times to one's own loss?

I have witnessed people who have excessive "work-obsessed" joys that become excessive pains with excessive laughter that becomes their sorrow. Without moderation and an innate know-how of our own limitations, we end up suffering things we do not need to suffer. Temporal peace can lead back to war on the self for many people. I prefer gravitating to a permanent peace that surpasses human understanding.

As the tall tree branches go with the order of the day, as the happy birds fly where their instinct leads them, and as the surprising buds spring up anywhere they are planted, we humans, too, move with our instinct once we have mastered our emotions and excessive desires. Bowing in worship to the Creator is as natural as breathing.

Do we choose peace, or do we choose war? For me, the answer is easy.

Worldly Religion

2005

When I went to the little Bible church,
I listened and cried alone in my pew
People embraced strange others
Like few I have seen do.
The wounds were open here,
And though I didn't live that history,
I felt free to let go and pray to God.
When I visited the temple with my gracious Sikh neighbor,
A college professor at Prairie View,
I knew God was around here, too.
Instead of watching the white-clad human in front,
I went back to Allah in my heart.
Long after prayer, I, too, shared in the laughter
And on the jokes on the human ego.
How frail we are.
When I said my prayers at the mosque,
Small enough to hear everyone's chats before prayers,
I breathed deeply, for I knew that
God was involved in our lives
Here and everywhere.
No, image around to divert my thoughts
On love's intellect, revealed to anyone who seeks love.

I don't want to drown in worldly religion
Nor pick and choose which commands to follow
that suit me...
In a time when doves bite the head of a turban
Or a star slays the crescent
Or the moon keeps a vigil on the hopeless
As some onlookers anywhere murder orphaned
children
At the drop of a hat or human command—
Or the bats in caves raise havoc
On the faceless thriving on diamonds or dope.
I'll take the fat off the old institutions
And skim my way back to faith.

Praying after a Nightmare

2000

I'm not free of wrath
I'm not cleansed of sin
Allah, make me whole
Allah, cleanse our names

I'm not cleansed of rage
I'm not pure as child
Allah, make me real
Let the moody side smile

I'm not free of hate
I'm not washed from dust
Allah, let me learn
Some of your own free will

Let me find your shelter
In the rocks and trees
Let me find your love
In the friends I see

Let me not judge so much
That I murk your name
Let me ditch my rage
Let me pour my shame

Let me walk with those
Who love you all the way
To your light and back
Let me free my pain

We're not free of rage
We're not cleansed of wrath
Let us shirk no one
Who confides in you

Let me comfort those
Who are true to you
Let me love creation,
His gift from you

Let us purge this rage
Not take you in vain
Let us be like those
Who, for you, shall change

For our selfish ways
To healing ones
For you have always loved
Everyone who's gone

Let me hurt no one
Let me purge my wrath
Let me walk with those
Who befriend your grace

Let me be like those
Who have lived your word
Let me not doubt the teachers
Of your grace and will

Let me be cleansed of sin
Just like a newborn babe
Wipe my slate, Allah, throw my rage
Into the red, red sea

Let me be a source
That finds healing pain
I'm not free of wrath
I'm not yet cleansed of rage
Ameen

Andalusia

2004

The olive grove above the hills
Is not the same as other groves here—
Its fruit, though plump and dark, is acrid;
Its dry-dusty earth, barren now.
There is a road along that grove
Where *gitanos* mourned—roaming souls
Who lost their gold from land to land,
Shedding ghostly tears, feeling no more,
Remembered by the swaying reeds.

Some say the gypsy shout is stout and loud
And echoes in hollow caves, resounding—
Scattered noises in the wind
Of times long gone and days long lost—
Today, we climbed the vacant hill
And witnessed nestled in the land
Legends of woe-begotten souls,
Whose olives are strewn upon the ground,
Whose bitter seeds are present still—
The olive groves upon the hills.
Those olive groves upon the hills.

My Haven on Earth

2005

When I was seventeen, without a car or confidante
But a few good friends who sheltered me,
I'd go down to the Ozark waters
Or find a ride to Hickory Creek.
Some evenings I'd sit with both feet plopped on rock,
Watch local children fishing, water chiming in.
Geology class was over, but I'd study the rocks
And roam around, seeing which ones were sedimentary,
Which ones, igneous.
In Queens, I'd rarely take the subway, not too sure of where to
    go alone,
But I kept the memory of Hickory Creek past the twenties and
    thirties
Until I'd dream of the Ozarks again.
In Trenton State, I met the poet Lahna Diskin, eyes like goblets,
    deep and brown,
In Fayetteville, a laughing Derek Walcott sharing lines from the
    West Indies, reminiscing.
In Lahore, Faiz Ahmad Faiz kissed me on the temple.
With a prayer as Ammi thanked him,
In Dallas, Billy Collins lit the fire again, jolly near two-hundred—
A few lines here and there,
Traveling everywhere with rugged freedom.
Mt. Vernon and the honeymoon heritage taught me domesticity,

Teaching in a green and scented farming community
How to tender knowledge-seeking souls, how to wear my
    shroud of peace,
Receiving the beaded sanctuary between my Easternness
And Westernness, the highs and lows of either never having
    mattered.
Ten steps toward the center, ten steps back,
In all the talks with teachers of delight: Abbey Clark and Sharon
    Schmaeling,
Taking our language, leaning into aerobics after schooling,
Weimmer, Regieck, McGroy, Steven Crossen, Bernie,
Jyung Ae-Cho—exposure to certain femininity
But never wore its dress too boldly.
Oh, daughter of the freedom thinkers and the martyrs, the
    engineers,
The chefs and prime ministers, historians, landlords, doctors,
Teachers, shepherds of Almighty, poet police officers, homemakers,
White sari-ed ladies, women orators, the contented, the
    passionate,
The grief-stricken, the joyous, the migratory, the steadfast,
The praisers of Allah, the mixed descent,
The criticized, the liberal, the misaligned, the branching,
The conservative, the critic, the sisters paying homage to each
    other—
A fusion of all loving hearts into one sibling race—
Sikh and Arab, Muslim, Christian, Turk, or Jew,
Bodhisattva or Confucian, desert saints or wild sage
With leaves growing from his back
Chanting love is great, God is great, God is love—
Daughters of egalitarian men and women,
Freethinking people of each creed renowned,
Do you really see your privileged face today?
What race?
Just a pulse, a beating of good hearts,

A clot of blood from semen drops,
A human babe or anguished joy,
waiting to be born
Lovers of God, of humans, and of friends,
Mothers waiting to love each child being born.

On Finding
Someone's Old Report Card
Human Natures

2005

Strange that the yellowed report card I found on page 10 of *Far from the Madding Crowd* may as well be as old as Hardy himself.

I'm supposed to have reread that book by now just before teaching from it,

But like the first reader, I had to find the first cause.

Existence of Hardy's essence, I knew somehow.

All the ancient buildings, churches, and road descriptions before the plot even begins to begin His themes of heroines with substance and tenacity...

But I was left off on page 10 too in this rereading,

Wondering why you, Roberta Myers, did not connect with Bethsheba,

Landowner, stronger heroine of Hardy's novels,

Or her resistance to handsome Gabriel instantly.

And why are Hardy's male figures so hard to read anyway?

Gabriel, the most angelic?

Let's see here: a *C* in American government,

A *C+* in Bible 2, a *B* in English,

(You had a hard year), and grade 42 for Mr. Coffin's class.

I note your student number was E5120 in the year '83.

Too much information has leapt onto my lap from Half Price
    bookstore.
They didn't unwrap as I read into your school life.
Good Roberta Myers with much to do,
We must be the same age group, too, Roberta,
From Corpus Christi school, when we daydream upon our
    readings,
We reflect on all whom learning's leaving out then and now.
Where are you now?
Do you work, paint, bake cookies, or teach?
Are you far away from the maddening crowd of learners?
I have one here in class next to me who seeks to complete
    another Hardy novel.
Most have finished and written their responses,
But someone's still reading on, a quiet one with good intentions.
What page will the next Hardy readers leave Hardy on?

Why Do We Teach Anyway?

Service is the rent we pay to live on earth.
—Muhammad Ali

*There are some people who prefer to look
their destiny straight in the eye.*
—Albert Camus

June 24, 2021

In contradictory times, why do we still teach? Why do we require our students to think for themselves instead of handing them worksheets to complete in college campuses or expect students to listen to our lectures and discussions? Our learning audience is as important as the variety of materials we use for teaching. Our communicative patterns are as significant as what we don't say in the classroom. And what we don't say in the classroom about our understanding of our students' identities is as important as what we do say because our students will inevitably trust us based on how we perceive them and our regard to their potentialities.

How consistent can we be in letting students figure out how to use the materials we share with them in our various classes? This group wants us to teach this-a-way, and that group wants us to teach that-a-way. And there we go, losing half the class for listening to everybody else but the students' intellectual, socio-emotional, and career-driven needs.

After all, don't we instructors know that half the class will be silently distracted on their cell phones, underneath the cumbersome notes that we, in our dreams, hope someone is taking during class.

Notes? What notes? A student in my Lone Star College class would joke whenever I would hint that it is notetaking time, and we would be tested on the material in different forms. What notes? Those notes, not the cell phone notes.

We still teach because we need people (and we read people) who can objectively see aspects of students that no family member has ever seen before or that they themselves never saw in themselves before. We teach because we were that student at some point in our lives when we sat, taking notes and wondering why we are doing this anyway and what's to become of us in the future after this subject and that subject. When we instructors look back on the successes of students' lives and career drives, we are reminded of good businesses that began from scratch: both required hours and hours of self-belief, tenacity, perseverance, and the discovery of potential despite all odds. Perhaps we instructors came from situations that challenged us intellectually and emotionally, and still we succeeded despite all odds.

From five different college campuses, one unusually diverse high school—diverse in thought before cultures—and five different teaching jobs, I found one concept in common in all of these realms: communicating with consistency never fails to lead students astray from their goals or from themselves. Too many students of ours will have witnessed vast inconsistencies in their previous lives' communicative patterns. Let us be the exception to their rule of contradictions in trust.

Today we live in an era when few people know whether to believe people or not no matter how lofty their speeches or how savvy their humor. Maybe too often, people fail to provide evidence for giving people their trust. And fewer people seem to have a sense of normalcy in their lives. What seemed normal behavior just ten years ago seems abnormal today. For example, ten years ago, we would not have imagined going into any class and seeing students become "fresh" with their technologies and choosing to decline the assignments we instructors are offering them for practice-based skills, let alone enrichment. Now it seems that giving students demanding assignments that challenge their thinking patterns is a lot to ask. We seem to have given up on our own thinking capabilities and rely more and more on group chats, political venues, and educational clichés that take our students nowhere.

Sometimes we instructors are expected to perform miracles in the classrooms as nurses are expected to perform daily miracles in the overcrowded hospitals. Without student preparation (or patient/client preparation), we go at our work alone, knowing full well that the more of a lonership we take in serving our students' needs (clients' needs), the riskier it is for an active communicative base. Today each word we speak matters—how we say it, to whom we say it, and why we say it—as we prepare quite ahead of time for each of our classes so that no one disconnects with the class's larger communication base. We are taking in students who have come from dysfunctional careers, broken-home situations, situations of violence, and out-of-state or international students with traditions as rich in nuances as our own range of linguistic nuances. To be trusted by our students, we have to be trustworthy and trust ourselves in the range of techniques we offer our variety of learners. We have to be available on levels beyond the cognitive symbols. Now we need to be empathic and clinical yet detached to be professional while adapting to their changing realities. We need to be authoritative in our subjects without coming across as authoritarian so as not to lose the students who need a friendlier approach. We need to be cautious in not using offensive language to our students who are often very sensitive to educators' biases and ivory-tower extraordinaire in not understanding where are students are coming from. Simultaneously, we need to fulfill the obligations of the current curriculum as mandated by the college and not do things on a whimsical basis too often so as not to lose the trust of our students who expect some kind of routine in their chaotic, busy lives.

Thus, we continue seeking to balance our own knowledge base with enough material to allow students to understand the subjects without stepping on their boundaries. We need to be well-versed in their lingo so as not to forget the generational gaps between instructors and pupils. At the same time, we are teaching students to rise above their difficult circumstances while using academic language to support their ideas in an increasingly political and diverse climate of extreme polarization. How do we manage such a seemingly impossible position? By overconfidence? No. By a pal system of select students to whom we largely communicate in each course? Of course not. By refusing to share any analogical input from our own travel or reading experiences? No.

Learners need our authenticity without an added animus to the classroom. In short, we have to be ready for anything and everything at every single class period, and that includes being mentally agile enough—as Mr. Sanderson was during the Columbine mass shooting—for any violent outbreak that can occur in any university campus at any given time. This means that we are to prepare our students to be mentally and emotionally ready (fitness is their own responsibility, not the teacher's) to go beyond the learning experience that matches their career goals; rather, we need to treat students as though they were an extension of our global and national family so that they can also treat their fellow students with the same respect, care, and professionalism at all times. Mr. Sanderson, after all, did not require gun ownership in the classroom to act responsibly while saving the lives of his students, whom he was in charge of during teaching hours. Mr. Sanderson's faith was enough to let him take the necessary risks to do the right thing without blinking once. As we know, faith with true works can produce miracles in many cases.

Why do we teach in times that are so inconsistent and polarized? To have some continuity of our democracy through the varied and rich heritages that we all share without letting some students feel lost, uncomfortable, or blamed for the past efforts that have brought this country to where we are today. And getting lost in other people's ideologies is especially detrimental for any instructor who seeks to connect with all students despite our differences in class, race, gender, ethnicity, traditions, etc. As a mathematician colleague of mine used to say during our writing hours together, "Doesn't everybody have some kind of agenda? Even not having an agenda is an agenda!" Of course, David was a very funny person, and despite our generational and cultural and philosophical differences, we got along just fine during all of our writing times. This required backing off, staying detached, and closely listening to the other person's perspective. Good communication between diverse communities in the classroom requires close listening skills and more nodding and acknowledgement than voicing our opinions. After all, it is the students' classroom, isn't it? Who are we to keep talking once we have facilitated the presentation or lecture with various techniques to keep them entertained?

For me, diversity is more about thought differences rather than superficial, geographical origin distinctions; however, having said that, I believe we must honor each of our separate identities in the classroom and outside of the classroom because, even when our students and faculty are not there with us, their presence is consistently with us through the daily exchanges that we will have inevitably shared throughout the semester. To honor a few students' identities over the other students is a weak strategy, not to mention careless and insensitive. To honor all students' identities and heritages while knowing their traditions and perceptions about themselves is to begin adding the most important ingredient in any environment: personal comfort for a diligent and resourceful outcome for all concerned.

Carrying Our Truth in
Our Own Hearts

*Do not make mischief on earth, after it hath
been set in order, but call on Him with fear
and longing (in your hearts): for the Mercy of
Allah is (always) near to those who do good.*
                          —Sura "The Heights"

*But as for those whose hearts pursue their desire
for abhorrent acts and detestable practices, I
will bring their conduct down on their own
heads. This is the declaration of the Lord God.*
                          —Ezekiel

June 30, 2021

When I was younger, trying to seem sophisticated and worldly,
I really did think that truth was relative to one's experience and attitudes. In some ways, I can still join those conversations if necessary
and if I have to; otherwise, arguing for the sake of argument is not
my cup of tea (or coffee).

But suffering combined with depression over situations beyond
my control has taught me that my truth is more important than ever
before, and who I am and how I find contentment despite the misery
around me in the larger society matters more than ever before.

As someone who has contributed in meaningful ways to the
larger society but feels like one of Camus's Arabs in his essays and
novels in a country that practices "freedom for all and dignity for all

people" is like breathing through the gallows while living as long as I am able. This does not mean that I will ever depend on the wrong people should I have grave needs, nor does it mean that I shall give up my way of life so that a society that is largely anti-Muslim feels good about itself. But we accept everyone as they are, the positive optimists will say, many without practicing those sentiments.

Thus, truth that anyone practices from their said creed shall matter more to me than anyone who talks "truth" but does nothing about said "truth."

I have even heard certain speakers declare publicly, "Why do some people make their lives harder than God makes their lives?" and such people have not suffered or been subjected to societal harms or large betrayals of human trust. It never made sense to me when certain people go out of their way to make others' external lives miserable for no justifiable reasons, for I would never do the same to such people. For me, that statement about making one's life harder than God makes it has an inherent flaw: that we humans are not responsible for how we live and treat others. We are responsible to use our particular truth to do good deeds on earth in a conscious manner at every second of our lives; the second we err on the wrong side of our own truth, we have become inconsistent in what call our truth. There is nothing wrong with seeking perfection in our deeds for the sake of God alone. When we falter from doing good deeds, it is our responsibility, not God's responsibility, to erase and wipe out everything that we did wrong to people or to ourselves. "No bearer of burdens shall take the burdens of another" is an essential aphorism from Allah's guidance. This guidance gives us added responsibility in our lives not just to be keepers of good in our land, wherever we live, but also to be our brother and sister's keepers (as the Bible has taught before).

The Quran's concept of responsibility for one's truth and assertion of one's truth—"There is no God, but Allah; and Muhammad is His (Final) Prophet"—means that we act according to the examples set before us even while accepting our frailties and weaknesses as imperfect human beings. The Quranic guidance tells thinkers who love God that, despite earthly provocations and misery, He gives us what we can handle, and with every difficulty, there is relief. The phrase "There is relief" is repeated twice, possibly to remind us that we need to find that silver lining in everything we are suffering even if we think that silver lining is not there on earth or in the skies, leading toward heavenly ways of justice and peace on earth rather than man's vacillating attempts to make peace and justice remain on earth. The stoic, Christian literary example of *Jane Eyre* reminded me of a tough yet soft Muslim woman when I first read Charlotte Bronte's rendering of her character: generous with no one to understand her deeply, real but in a world that seemed a facade, true to her God but always journeying without having perfect answers for everything, and abused often by people who did not understand her artistic nature. Yet she persisted in our truthful journey without relying on anyone with pretty talks and inappropriate invitations to India, for that was not her calling. She was clean and true to her self-worth without being tainted by people who lived messy lives.

In real life, Malala is another example of someone true to her truth; I am not one of those Pakistani Americans who callously describe Malala as being tainted by commercial successes. She lives what she believes, and her success came largely from defending herself and her educational passion from the harsh, maniacal, and patriarchal Taliban; Allah seems to have given her people's trust in England/Oxford, who truly understood her cause. That England is the England I remember—where I could walk on lovely, scenic, and unruly streets going up miles and miles to the small cheese pasty shop for a cup of English tea and conversations with the locals while never being disturbed for being a complex person of similarly diverse character. The six months or so that I lived in England at my beloved mother-in-law's home was when I distinctly practiced my truth and found myself living in perfect harmony with my outside environment, though I had not yet suffered as deeply as I had from 2016 onward.

Those who have lived more privileged lives often want to advise people who have not lived privileged lives by giving them examples from their truth, which does not make logical sense to those of us who do contribute to society and family life in meaningful ways without distinguishing between the classes of people that society likes to make up.

Once I had a Sikh friend, a college professor with whom I would occasionally walk in my old neighborhood. She had taught English literature and composition classes at Prairie View University, and each evening, we would check on each other's way of life out of respect for one another. Not once did either one of us attempt to change the other person's point of view in how we chose to live our separate but equal lives or how we gained our livelihood. Both of us were very happy in our chosen career domains while teaching in secular and "then-equal" teaching environments.

I came to realize that while my professor friend had a diverse way of life and while her truth was distinct from mine and my chosen lifestyle, we had more in common than the differences that people who are nonthinkers like to make. It is similar to today's neighborhood friends who have diverse ways of life and distinct truths that seem to help them manage their lives just fine. Neither one of us attempted to argue with the others' perspectives for argument's sake or whatever other reasons to bring us over to another truth with slightly different meanings than our own.

Thus, while each person asserts his or her own journey in adhering to one's truth, each person, in an equal ambiance, even if it is a small ambiance, establishes the dignity of the other person's said truth.

With each of our truths—truth in the singular and truth in the plural in a diverse society, we cannot achieve communal harmony whether it is political harmony or religious or familiar harmony. Acceptance of people requires a full journey into their consciousness, not a partial one with ambiguously bigoted thoughts hindering their personalities based on the truth they have claimed.

Now I carry my truth within my heart without any hindrances whatsoever, and as Camus has said in his essays, when we do no harm to people, we carry a lighter conscience while existing for whatever purpose we have established. For me, that purpose is Allah. I live for His sake, and I shall die for His sake over any piece of ownership of either individual's or land or property. I am not owned by anybody, nor am I required to own anybody even in my marriage, which is a spiritual contract between two equal and spiritual partners. For Allah's sake was I created; for Allah's sake do I pay my service to fellow human beings, who He has created in His interest so that I can pay my "rent" on earth.

And this truth makes me free.

When Companies Mess Up Big-Time

When a land is in rebellion, it has many rulers,
but with a discerning and knowledgeable
person, it endures… When the righteous
triumph, there is great rejoicing, but when
the wicked come to power, people hide.
—Proverbs 28:2, 12

The one who sows injustice will reap disaster,
and the rod of his fury will be destroyed.
—Proverbs 22:8

Those who, when they have to receive by
measure from men, exact full measure,
but when they have to give by measure
and weight to men, give less than due.
—Sura "The Dealers in Fraud"

O my father, do not serve Satan: for Satan
is a rebel against Allah Most Gracious.
—Sura Mary/Maryam

June 29, 2021

When companies mess up,
They crave someone to blame—
One who doesn't kiss up to big-heads, or
Spread lies about their works and name

They crave a "smaller" punching bag,
As big nations do to smaller nations
All Japanese families interned
Instead of the few treacherous comrades

It must feel good for empty souls,
Demoralizing anyone working harder
Than they, not seeming part of greed schemes
Until someone, too, blames them soon

Their heads get wrung in ladder holes
For doing harm to people,
Climbing upward with shortcuts and hoes,
Falling soon, exposed

The biggest talkers with booming voices
Aren't always right with all their numbers
And precision isn't valued even if you even shake a finger,
Correcting things that need correcting

For someone will take credit
For works you've been directing,
Craving another slap on shoulders
Stiffened egos
Another raise, another profit
No matter how they got there

The Choices We Make

Do not walk the earth with arrogance.
—Holy Quran

Muhammad, (Peace be upon him), was an indulgent husband. He insisted that his wives live frugally in their tiny, sparse huts, but he always helped them with the household chores and looked after his own personal needs, mending and patching his clothes, cobbling his shoes, and tending the family goats. (They were poor but blessed. With Aisha particularly he was able to unwind, challenging her to footraces and the like. She had a sharp tongue and was by no means a shy or submissive wife, but she liked to spoil Muhammad, anointing his hair with his favorite perfume, and drinking from the same cup. One day, while they were sitting together, the Prophet busily repairing his sandals, she saw his face light up at a passing thought. Watching him for a moment, she complimented him on his bright, happy expression, and Muhammad, (Peace be upon him), got up and kissed her forehead, saying, "O Aisha, may Allah reward you well. I am not the source of joy to you that you are to me." Muhammad, (Peace be upon him), lived cheek by jowl with his family and companions and saw no opposition between his public and private life. [The scholar, may Allah's peace and mercy always be on her, went

from being a good nun to a religious and spiritual
mediator between religions and philosophies.]
    —Karen Armstrong, *Muhammad*

July 1, 2021

From water we come, and I believe
From dust we are made, and I believe,
Formed from the Highest's One's sublime imagination
How can we mere humans, with much nobility within,
Compare ourselves ever to the One Merciful
Who gives us FI is signals when we completely
Believe and fully submit to His eternal freedom,
Given so freely with just enough laws
To keep law and order on this still green earth
That some wish to destroy faster than darkness's
Trains whizzing over the hills?
Some braying ones think they made themselves
Or popped into the earth through some accidental burst
As if anyone is self-made, not even grand Satan,
Serpentine essence, crawling inside anyone,
Boasting and boasting how richly they made themselves
Without any need—only mead from earth's boisterous, brewing
        secret cosigners
Of darkest realms unseen (that keeps on catering to men's rest-
        less greed).
What is this "I" that we speak of again and again,
As if the good that humans have done on earth.
No one of glory has been near us since dawn,
The eyes that see, see what they'd like to believe,
Dozens of senses drowned by things that can be seen
And drunk, polluting are our gifts lent by the Divine,
His mercy that gives even when we want not to receive
As mothers keep giving when their children are done
For a while, that well-known Author we seek and find
In each desperate crisis when no one's around,

Giving and giving comfort and miracles
To whomever He pleases for whatever His reasons
Whenever we obey what we intrinsically know,
Coming back to Him, whom we've always known.

Here are those short poems I want to share when my dear husband, Khursheed Anwar (ray of the sun), can have breakfast conversations and prayer times as we had begun doing, enjoying our quiet moments in our marriage-sunset privately at home. I somehow know that he would finally enjoy some of these poems as he did in Illinois when we'd travel together to different states for his Bureau of the Budget job as we did here where he best loved his work friends and taught me to stop overindulging on my negative fears regarding persecution complexes due to my race. He taught me that I still need to be myself and not look here and there all the time worrying who might be following me. Khursheed, as he loves the people he learns from and works with, reminds me to give people the benefit of the doubt and trust the good inside fellow equal human beings who are simply working toward reaching their goals. This was how I used to be in my normal circumstances years ago. But now, my husband is in another state; and soon, we will be facing a newer journey together. I intend to keep his wisdom and empirical knowledge with me every day as I build back better, President Biden's term (pun intended), to attain the privilege of being the best version of myself for the sake of my beloved husband. Sometimes, we teachers have to learn to be nurses before we become teachers; other times, we transform into teachers from nursing and the medical field.

1a. *Poem 1: For Khursheed*

How many times did you drive, and I was sleeping?
How many times did you love me, and I wasn't feeling?
How many times did you take me far, and I wasn't thinking?
How many times did you give me sense, and I was numb?

How many times did you drive, and I was sleeping?
How many times did you love me, and I wasn't feeling?
At times we, women, are late, when we cannot wait.
Not wait for moments we dream that were always there.

How many times did you drive, and drive, and drive, and I was
    sleeping?
And how spoiled I was by your loving, constant loving, without
    ever needing to say
Those tainted three-letter words we women are counting?
And how quiet were you on all the words I was giving?

How many times did you speak that logic that I wasn't learning?
Love isn't words; it's thinking, feeling, doing.
And now I have to carry that logic that you'd been giving?
That love isn't words; it's thinking, feeling, doing.
That love isn't words; it's thinking, feeling, doing.

How many times did you love me, Khursheed, and I wasn't
    feeling?
How shallow are we, humans,—we know when someone mat-
    ters when they're sleeping?
My shallow shell broke loose when you were sleeping.
How many times you've loved me, and I wasn't knowing of all
    your varied love notes beyond recording?

May Almighty give us another chance to forget romance's
    demons—to love each other deeply "as I would love you
    still in heaven and earth" (Inshallah). Amen.

1b. So numb we are in every life's awakening that we don't even
look around to see Allah's grandeur, kindness, mercy, we don't even
look around to see each loving person that we meet. Yet new cre-
ations arise in creation's dawning as I understood the Quran says. We
are not the only ones. We humans are so absorbed in our little, idle
selves, numb to every single awakening, numb to every single bloom

that comes and goes. Even we—sleeping souls—have such small parallel universes inside ourselves, different versions of ourselves that come out after turmoil felt on earth.

Whatever we think, we know. We never ask "why did we live?" How little control we have though we think we have enough. Each little awakening, we get another chance to see something bigger out there than humans ever thought they'd get a glance at in the universe—a sign of life that we'd otherwise not see.

1c. I took the route to Eldridge because you told me to.
Baji's house road you told me to take for my own comfort.
I took the road you told me to.
Why ever take the roads not meant for me?
I didn't always respect the one—you—that Ammi taught me to.
Still, Allah kept on giving blessings from His well of mercies.
My favorite time, the Maghreb prayers, we shared together.
I took for granted every single thing you did for me,
A spoiled version of myself just as spoiled as those I criticized so
    distinctively.
You are my Rome, my Paris, and my New Delhi too.
I still take the roads most trusted that you told me to.
You are my logic, my finesse, my solid self-composure
that built its strength from what I saw in you.
You are my Rome, my Paris, and my New Delhi too.

1d. *Reminiscence at seven-seventeen, Khursheed Anwar's birthday,*
    our ray of bright sun

This is not Khursheed's last job. Let not it be, Ya Allah. Inshallah, by your mercy and grace, we will have another chance to show him how much we love him, not be words that he does not trust but by action; not by arguments, but hugs and compassion, tighter bonds, cuddling breakfasts, tea with embraces we both miss so much.

Each morning, Khurhseed, you'd wake up early after a midnight ride of remembrances of all accounts at work, making me coffee along with yours—swirling amid night swirls, checking on your

241

meetings and buddies at work for whom and with whom you'd set the highest standards so that all levels would be productive.

I thought I'd knew most everyone with your jubilant conversations on the telephone by name. I'd smile—still you'd word. How did you remember every detail of each memo? My mind does not work this way—all the levels would be productive, truly generous to each one with their critiques as well as bluntness. That's my job; you'd say to me.

We don't compliment people for everything they're supposed to do. (I sure learned that philosophy when the kids were young!) Your top-notch yet tough-loving Asian parent syndrome (APS).

Mr. Edwards lovingly calls "that statesman" to our son. You made a ninety-eight! How dare you! Make a one hundred. Go ahead! (Someone had to be the softer parent even if it came hard to me.)

At home, you'd set the highest standards of excellence—like Baji Tanveer—much like your personality on full-drive all the time.

No wonder she'd joke, "Khursheed is my relative more than you, Kausam." I didn't mind. So true. So true. I'm on another clime of another mindset—can be taken advantage of sometimes. Not you, my darling. Not you. You see through our cracks. Could have been that average good-enough teacher, popular and easy to keep around through tougher stances.

Do what you thought was impossible for your children and your students. Do it. Your motto. Now, I understand Allah does work in mysterious ways. How right the ancient revelations were too. Impossible can wear one down; it can be your persona sometimes. Still working through 1:30 a.m.? I'd tickle you, at times, so entwined you were on finishing up that task nicely.

I'd often like to slide into easier ways. A comfort-foodie too many times. You'd inspire blueberries and mangos in me. Still, you'd lead us all effectively, my beloved Khursheed. Do you forgive me as you sleep? I miss that tough Khursheed—the one who always had an answer for my confusions, my pathetic flaws in technology. How you taught me statistics, earning a B in Illinois State University, driving down to snow-capped streets from Normal University to Springfield. Dr. PanCRAZio was super-smart like you and super tough on me yet kind, reminding me of all the values she and I cherished together from our People of the Book ways as a devout Roman Catholic that she was charitable, logical, statistical, family-mannered like you.

And you kept on pushing the children to achieve the impossible in their voice, in their tasks, in their chores, and in their standards. People in their lives had to be tough and loving without needing to use that notorious word *love*, a word we poets love to use and misuse and misunderstand.

"Love you too." My elder cousins make fun of me each time I say it to my kids. "Spoiling them again?" And I know, you are from another generation—devoted more to deeds and talks. It was more about achievements than seeing splendor everywhere. Yet I now see, as Allah has me see, all the splendors in you, my dear, who are more American than I am in certain ways, as I have become more English and Eastern in certain ways than even you on which you were raised paradoxically. I suppose, this is what the marriage contract in Islam means: we take the best from each other and compromise what is weaker. I am still learning that part, but the promise is true; I will intend to be the better version of Kausam (as wife and friend) to you.

When the children were overwhelmed by your high expectations, I'd call you "Your Majesty" when I was angry at you passively-aggressively; and you'd retort with a condescending clarity, "Yes, Your Highness," implying that I need to shut up when you were talking to yourself about memorizing and foreseeing budgets at work or at home, reminding me that I was your spiritual equal, as it is in Quran, as I expected more chivalry from you—not seeing that you are who you are, and I am who I am. Acceptance of one another is better than expected admiration—short-lived.

For the kids, some faced with the "another Asian parent syndrome" when some of their buddies, not Asian, didn't have the crazy standards in whatever they were studying or inventing. Now, it shall be your turn all the time, my darling Khursheed.

You once wrote on an anniversary, before the brilliantly planned Puerto Rico and Egypt and Spain trips, that "you are my solid rock" to me. Well, let me tell you, you, Khursheed Anwar Salam, have been and still are my solid rock from which I held on to my morals and values and standards. We will be giving you all the embracing you deserved all along for which we were too passive sometimes.

How much I cherish (see, I did not say "Love, love me do" as your sweet-funny brothers, Anjum and Haidu, sing to you with Erum), how much I cherish all stages of you. Like your name that my Ammi—your best friend in our family, their Nanna—Khursheed Anwar, you are as bright as the hot, shining sun, I cherish you most of all and will find in me the nurse-before-the-teacher and the-friend-before-the-wife status until we get back to normal, Inshallah.

And yes, all of your loved family members and friends—all of them—have been coming to see you regularly in all four hospital setups, even Javed Sher Bhai with whom you'd stay up till odd hours in the morning, talking old politics and sciences; Kelly, whom you cherish; Dr. Khalida Baji; Yusuf and family with many, many prayers from the heart; Haseen Bhai and Nadeem; Dr. Neaz, whom even prayed by your side several times; the children; the young beloveds, Tim and Maliha, whom have been praying; your work buddies; Jeff, who loves you as a brother; Manjiri; Marcus; Mr. Edwards; and the rest that keep checking on you, Khursheed my darling, sending your family days of food offerings of love as our neighbors and Ms. Roxanne, whom you met several times and enjoyed her scones that she'd regularly prepare for you and me. Lali has visited as often as she can. Chama and Suboohi and Askari have called frequently checking on you. Fayyaz and Javed Bhai, whom you always enjoy conversing with in Long Island, checks on you. Sayeed Bhaiyya never fails to inquire about your mood and conditions. Fazal Chacha and Rifat Auntie (Akka's best friend in Philadelphia) made their home available to us; so did Shahida Baji and Sagir Bhair. And of course, we never take for granted the loving-kindness of Dr. Neaz Bhai and Baby Baji, just like brother and sister to us from day 1 in Texas when he himself was having surgery and still invited us indefinitely without expectation. Amen.

Your English friends are always checking on you also, Khursheed. Man! I thought I had some friends. Who did I think I was? Your friends and buddies from younger days are tighter with you than siblings today!

244

Yup, you sure are right, Khursheed. Love and friendship do not need songs, poems, and words. Action and commitment to all relationships were made by Allah for us as you'd teach me in the early days when we'd visit Tanveer and Dr. Khursheed Malick's family whom we both love dearly even to this day. Even the kids' uncle Khalid called you though he is far away. My friends Kathie, Nadine, Annette, Rashida, Ms. Love, and the team check on you. Ms. Reed checked on you.

I have so much to read as you heal, but this is my reminiscence of this part of our third journey after turmoil. You have some of the warmest yet most clinical nurses, doctors, and therapists at your side, including home people training themselves to become speech people too. (Daughter). Our son calls regularly and checks on you as does our daughter-in-law, and Mariam checks on me for your sake so that I may be equipped to take better care of priorities by the mercy of Allah.

May Allah forgive us any small or uncalled for digressions. May Allah help us heal together, and may our family come together again in wondrous ways. Amen.

> This is my servant. I strengthen him. This is my chosen one. I delight in him. I have put my Spirit on him. He will bring justice to the nations. He will not cry or shout or make his voice heard in the streets. He will not break a bruised reed.(Isaiah)

> Allah has created every living creature from water. (Holy Quran)

> A lie—that we come from water. The truth is we were born from stones, dragons, the sea's teeth, as you testily, with your crust and jagged scissors. (Margaret Atwood)

For mammals with their lobes and bulbs,
scruples and warm milk, you've nothing but
contempt.

Dear poetic heart,
With all the jewels inside your words, etched before your Maker,
who made you with so much grace,
Carved you with such wonder, life gives us women awful things
of substance to deal with, and how we deal with our sub-
stantive analysis
With all the wisdom we think we have inside us, carving out
a better place for us women, men, and children—mam-
mals—than what that patriarchy has given us.
So I prefer the foolish role of giving the benefit of doubt to the
Lord, who lets us climb out of this frozen shell into something
We ourselves cannot believe.
Sure, men of the world have given us fear from beyond ourselves,
Terror inside our wombs about what they think we are.
Let us rise above the crawling critters we have been portrayed
to be,
Still beautiful in their own ways, bellies across the seas, reaching
toward our spiritual destinies, Where we don't have to
climb anymore
Or clamber across the gulfs to save ourselves from deities' tar-
geting words.

July 1, 2021
Survivors, All of Us, Until We Don't

The Sea of Faith was once, too, at the full,
and round earth's shore lay like the folds of a
bright girdle furled. // But now I only hear / its
melancholy, long, withdrawing roar, / retreating,
to the breath / of the night-wind, down the vast
edges drear / and naked shingles of the world.
　　　　　　　　　　　　　　—Matthew Arnold

Faith was virtually gone from the Victorians' lives
Imagine how little faith we have now in the postmodern times.
When using faith-based ideals, we glide across our highways,
Forgetting why we are or our own purpose to shine our separate
　　　rays,
Given by that same One who gives to all,
As we misplace our own existence
For cravings, one after another, after another,

Never tiring of this world's bold substitutes of seraphic
　　　luminescence.
"Have faith," we say to each other in crisis times.
When our Maker heals the day,
Still we say our faith on something made us survive the dangers
Of any outside realm.

What if faith is all we had and nothing else—not fame, not
bread, not drink, not warmth, not shelter, not anything to show for

how we've worked, not popularity, not honor from people, not even wisdom, not even a basic comfort, not even family or friends who cared consistently, not even love that we think we have a right to, not even job security, not confidence, not looks anymore, not excessive energy, not laborious effort as we used to have? What then?

This could be that time when everything we thought we knew about our rights on earth are shaken? And what we didn't know comes to question us again and again.

About existence? Faith in what?

Faith in whom? Faith in ourselves, by ourselves, for how long?

Faith in each other, in all we trust, until we can trust no more?

Faith in the prophets? In the Maker of angels? In the Maker of devils who keep persuading there is no devil, no "*makkar*," no Santa gliding from a chimney to a bar, faith in animal creatures who can suddenly change, shifting shapes into other beings? What then?

How shaky is our human faith.

How substantive our ways of letting material things take place, Of who we say believe.

And who rescues us from ourselves when we've got shaky faith?

Oh, Matthew Arnold, how right you were: without the sea of faith,

All we do is drown, sooner or later

Erasing ourselves before our enemies erase us.

Our Age-Long Concerns

Oh, if we draw a circle premature, heedless of far gain, / greedy for quick returns of profit, sure bad is our bargain! / Was it not great? Did not he throw on God (he loves the burthen)— / God's task to make the heavenly period perfect the earthen? / Does not He magnify the mind, show clear just what it all meant? / He would not discount life, as fools do here, paid by installment. / He ventured neck or nothing—heaven's success found, or earth's failure…this low man, goes on adding one to one, his hundred's soon hit: / this high man, aiming at a million, (pupils' progress), misses an unit. / That, has the world here—should he need the next, let the world mind him! // This, throws himself on God, and un-perplexed seeking shall find him. / So with the throttling hands of death at strife, ground he at grammar; / still, through the rattle, parts of speech were rife: while he could stammer… Here's the top peak; the multitude below live, for they can, there: / this man decided not to live, but know—bury this man there?
—Robert Browning, *A Grammarian's Funeral* (1854)

June 8, 2021

No, we teachers and grammarians
Never worked for big old money, just enough to make ends meet,
Never caring much for frivolities
That superior types keep on keeping on;
We never cared for big-shot fad programs
That shone a light on some, oppressing the rest,
Or followed those who only promote some extroverted
Types for their own social continuity—no.
We never cared too much for golden tokens
That take from tokenized veterans with new despair.
We only cared to teach all students
No matter who they were,
No matter from where they rose.

High potential still resides in each heart
Through whichever field they centered on
Until our tired brains had understood them.
We teachers never wondered how or where
Some wasted grants or monies that seemed to come
From air—whichever football fields or cheerleading
Triumphs there were—but academics, we sure knew were
Verging on architectural ruins
In anthropological landmarks crumbling down
From foundations we thought would last as long
As history, literature, music, the arts,
Or any field that suffers when it is substituted
For fads that come in rows off and on.

The Miraculous Power of Prayer

Truly, man was created very impatient; fretful
when evil touches him; and miserly when good
reaches him. No so those devoted to Prayer.
—Sura 70

A *church with a palm tree: In summary, at this*
ancient church called Kathisma, we seem to have
a tradition that depicts Mary with a miraculous
water spring and a palm tree with dates—the
very two elements found in both Pseudo-Matthew
and the Quran. That is truly remarkable...the
Protoevangelium of James, whose parallels with
the Quran we have seen, also says something
about the Nativity of Jesus, [Peace be upon him].
But remarkable, it does not place his holy birth
in Bethlehem, as it is located in the gospels of
Matthew and Luke and in the popular Christian
imagination. It rather places it in the wilderness,
somewhere between Jerusalem and Bethlehem.
Actually, in a cave exactly in the "middle of the
road." In other words, exactly the area where the
Kathisma church is. So, one wonders, could the
Kathisma church actually be the place at which
Mary (Peace be upon Hazrat Maryam) gave
birth to Jesus (Peace be upon him)? [I could not
stop reading this insightful research cover to cover
more than twice and would love to visit that exact
place where Jesus, peace be upon him, was born to

*Blessed Mary, peace be upon her, and their entire
family. Ameen.] She pointed towards him. They
said, "How can a baby in the cradle speak?"*
—Mustafa Akyol, *The Islamic Jesus:
How the King of the Jews Became
a Prophet of the Muslims*)

*He said, "I am the servant of God, He has
given me the Book and made me a Prophet.
He has made me blessed wherever I am and
directed me to do prayers and give alms as long
as I live, and to show devotion to my mother.
He has not made me insolent or arrogant. Peace
be upon me the day I was born, and that the
day I did and the day I am raised up again
alive." That is Jesus/Isa, son of Mary, the word
of truth about which they are in dispute.*
—Sura Maryam

If this is my last piece in this book, then so be it. Writing can be tiresome at times when speaking is much easier after reading pages and pages for years on a vast number of subjects. Yet I feel the need to still write as strongly as I felt the need to teach despite all odds in my topsy-turvy life.

I have had many uncertainties (as we all have experienced) at most points in my life's journey. We never know how long our comfort levels anywhere will remain steady; that does not mean that we become unsteady.

The gift of a variety of human emotions can unsteady anyone in times of uncertainty; however, the greater gift of Almighty God teaching us to pray gives us so much more than we ever bargained for in this world where showmanship matters more than personal achievements of any kind.

Once we give our lives over to God Almighty, who we call Allah, then anything can happen. This I knew since I was four years old, free to examine the varied rock textures and colors in our Chicago backyard. The trust that my parents gave me at such an early age allowed me to explore more than one terrain: the physical reality; the emotional realities that go up and down with life situations; the mind's reality as we asked questions about who made such and such and why that Reality would make us; and of course, the spiritual reality whenever I would see my father or mother praying anywhere, taking breaks from routine to remember the One who gave them everything they needed to live.

Of course, as stubborn as I am, I had questioned God's existence or His mercies from time to time in crisis situations during my late teenage years, and that was easy to do when so many young people did not make it their purpose to understand the nature of God in relation to ourselves and our needs. But each time I read something the agnostic thinkers would write, a sign would come to me about Almighty God's great existence: his mesmerizing palette that artists use for their imagination and his rewards and punishments, which we ascribe to human beings, simplifying our thought process.

When I think of how little Maryam, peace be upon her, was regarded at a certain point and how much God gave her in all possible blessings, I think of her ability to pray for long hours as God Almighty kept giving her one miracle after another, fulfilling her thirst and hunger with the most miraculous and healing gift of all: the miracle of birthing Jesus, peace be upon him, through virginal birth.

Who are we, then, to ignore the powers of prayer? Who are we to ignore the benign being who gives us much, much more than we could ever imagine we could possibly have in this earthly life (e.g., a place to live; a place to be ourselves as much as we allow ourselves comfort; compassionate family members; our spouse; our children; our friends; our health; and our ability to think, walk, talk, eat, drink, share, teach, love, hope, resolve conflicts, etc.).

We are certainly not a mistake. We are able to surpass almost any difficulty with which God is testing us, and surely, we can make life easier for fellow human beings when we are surpassing our own tests and shortcomings.

It is a miracle that Almighty God has shone down on us for centuries and centuries, allowing us humans of all races and traditions to build things based on the faculties he has bestowed on us, to communicate in so many verbal and nonverbal languages for good causes, to travel widely and see how fellow human beings live, to give birth to children who do good on earth, to write, to read, to make peace between families and each other... Surely, I, at least, could never have done all these things by myself alone.

If I could pray with enough energy more than five times a day, I would be grateful, but we only have to manage five—that is all—to keep realizing that we are more worthy and purposeful than what we allow ourselves credit for and that His grace is enough to keep the heart fulfilled when we have fully given our hearts back to God alone. Whether we get tons of rewards or a few punishments along the way, at least the soul knows that we are headed in the right direction.

Ameen.

Vignettes and Poems from Poet Nuzhat Alam

Translations from Urdu

Mrs. Nuzhat Alam, born on February 14, 1942, my mom's best school and college friend, was born in Patna, India. She migrated to Pakistan for a better life when wars that had begun between former friends (Hindus and Muslims) had turned part of the nation chaotic. Her husband, Faiz Alam, best friend and spouse of a blessed arranged marriage in 1967, India-chartered accountant, and she took courage and tried for a more comfortable life until they discovered the possibility to move to a still more comfortable life in London, England, where they lived happily for many years.

In London, two sons were born to them, giving them even greater blessings to look forward to. For a short while, Nuzhat Alam (Auntie) and Uncle Faiz moved to Scotland. Theirs had become a modern nomadic lifestyle as they enjoyed each stay in each land. In a job interview in Scotland, Nuzhat, Auntie, recalls that she kept saying, "No, I haven't," to almost every question, and due to her honesty and enthusiasm, which were evident in her "I will try any interesting job" outlook, she received an appointment letter a week later.

Her duties included working for a record office in which she had to make the conscientious decision about which criminal or ordinary citizens' files to keep or to destroy. This required patience, careful thinking, and knowledge of characters based on files studied. She shared with me, "Your uncle never asked me work," "To work was purely my choice," and that she was "proud of myself [herself] for becoming independent in the United Kingdom, a much different lifestyle than being a magistrate's daughter and well connected in the province of Bihar, from where the two friends met—my mom and she. On the side, however, almost every day, she wrote poetry and short stories, as writers everywhere are doing at this moment.

Finally, after a fun and entertaining lifestyle in the United Kingdom, still keeping most of their values systems including the courage to experience new lands, the two moved to the United States of America, where Uncle's career took off; and they enjoyed a still more comfortable lifestyle as the children grew up.

These poems and vignettes are written by a conscientious and loving mom as well as a scholar of Urdu literature (hers is a master's in Urdu from Karachi University, where I was lucky to visit with an Arkansas doctoral student–friend years ago).

Aunt Nuzhat continued writing in every interval of her life's journey. Sometimes my mom, also a lover of literature, would share her pieces with me as I grew up, loving English and Spanish literature while learning more about Urdu language, as she would recite poems, stories, and parables.

I am happy to share Auntie Nuzhat's writing with fellow lovers of literature and world experience. My aunt may not realize how much I am learning from her while recollecting all the stories and poems my mom would share with me as we grew up together, as all families grow up together when they listen to one another's stories.

As an added excitement to this project, when I began working on this phone-sharing a couple of weeks ago, my mom came in a dream as if looking down happily on me with joy in remembering her true friend from her school days. She was smiling, wearing a sea-green outfit, and it was as if still thirty-five, floating between earthly mountains and heavenly spheres. I can still see my Ammi visiting me as if giving me her go-ahead. Who knew that someday I might dare to translate her best friend's poems and stories that she was often fondly shared with me? Allah sends down inspiration in the most interesting ways even when my aunt never asked me to read her memorable works. In translations, as we know, much may be lost from the original language while moods may be captured depending on the depth and breadth of an image. As I honor my aunt's works, I seek to understand where she is coming from and how she adjusted on American soil after successfully raising her well-educated, well-traveled family.

Contents

1. The Lady Eternally Waiting by the Wayside in London Town.................................261
2. Ma Ki Dua: A Mother's Prayer 263
3. Barood aur Gulzar: Bombs Bursting from Flowers.............265
4. Chand Meray Ainay mai Karwaten Badalta: The Moon in My Reflection Keeps Changing Her Posture ...266
5. Azmaish: Examination.......................................268
6. In the Desert, a Metropolis Rose 270
7. Aeena Kiyoon Na Doon Kae Tamashaa Kaheen Jisay: The Outlandish Scenes of Brouhaha that the Mirror Shows...272
8. Zara 277
9. In a Quaint, Tiny Town.....................................278
10. Geet of the Masoom Era: Childhood Sojourning 279

The Lady Eternally Waiting by the Wayside in London Town

A Short Fiction Based on Observation

1972, London

It is an ordinary sight that I am speaking about. I see a lady from my flat as a shadow from my kitchen across to her kitchen. Her movements are ordinary; her life, extraordinary. But no one knows. No one sees her as I see her move about in her grim reality of living alone, entirely alone. Even the mail carrier on his fast-moving bike does not seem to meet her gaze, doing his busy, hard work and moving along about his business.

Perhaps she has grandchildren somewhere, children somewhere, who may have forgotten her living presence, the shelter that she has inside. Perhaps they see themselves somewhere as secure enough not to need an elderly lady among them anymore. This lady, so elderly, seems to have in her a bit of all of us somewhere at some time. What does she wait for? For whom does she make all of these gestures, moving and swaying about her way? Her hands are shaking. Her glances are downcast. Her waist has dropped almost to the floor.

Maybe she is the beloved of some precious children who see her once a year and gather around her as good workers gather around an empire. Maybe she holds them in her secure lap as a reflection of what hope looks like to them in a world where hope is torn from people.

My younger brother, Anwar, says, "*Yay bhuryiaa, sukoon bhi jeetnaa chaahati hai?*" (Doesn't she deserve her peace and privacy?). I do not listen to him as I go about doing my chores of the day for my family while reflecting on the lady directly across from me.

"Close off the drapes, Appi [older sister], so that you don't have to see her life."

Again, I do not listen, as her life is a part of all lives. All lives have mattered since the beginning of eternity. Who knows how her people, her own family, might see her or treat her? I wonder. Has she done some unpopular small sin that they decided not to be near her? From my window, a lady or grandmother is a source of life, a force to be reckoned with after living a long life, and someone who is or can be an entire edifice by herself. But out of fear or being unusual myself in a strange, new place, my own windows of reflecting have been opened wider for me.

But this regal, elderly lady across the flat from me is moving along the window's propinquity as if to make her presence known, doing her works neatly and tidily. Or perhaps how content she is, or might be, for years upon years of living solitarily in this same way, moving about and doing chores with dignity.

Ma Ki Dua A Mother's Prayer

1972

(*Nazm*/free style)

Do you even know, my Lord, do you *even know?*
My beloved God, Hiroshima has been taken out of the face of
    the earth.
Nagasaki has been turned to powder.

How did the war in Vietnam ever end?
Who have died? How many lived speaking louder and louder?

Oh my beloved Allah, do you not see what people are doing to
    people?
Bangladesh has bathed in its own blood.
How many generations are destroyed, my Lord?

How long will Hindustan and Pakistan live as enemies, my
    Lord?
How much do the children need to know?

Oh my children, do you even need to know
How much people are killing each other for all the borders that
    do not show?

How many innocents' funeral processions are going by?
How much warm blood has dripped and dried?

Today, the hand of friendship extends.
Who knows which hands of friendship will mend all of us, my
      Lord,
Flowing in the blood of humanity?

And how will the children learn to grow?
How much do the children need to know?

Barood aur Gulzar
Bombs Bursting from Flowers

May 2014,

Too often I sit here, thinking to myself,
How do we keep flowers from turning into bombs?

Children in cages, separated from their mothers
Gardens upon gardens made from single flowers upon flowers

A happy little child-flower, *what does he know?*
The blessings of mother and father inside him

As no one listens to the floral bud inside him
Precious little buds whose voices are suppressed

Is anyone listening out there?
What will become of these flowers without any care?

How do we take these small bombs of flowers
And reverse them back to their original shapes
Instead of bomb-flowers bursting, being exploited,

Separated from the ones who gave them care,
As every gardener nourishes his flowers,
Each one diverse from the others' bloom?

Chand Meray Ainay
mai Karwaten Badalta
The Moon in My Reflection
Keeps Changing Her Posture

*I know why you stare at the mountain's beauty, /
for she reminds you of something vital in yourself
/and natural desires to explore her heights are
just / there to help you reach your own summit.
/ Once, while I was looking at the sky, it
spoke, saying, / Hafiz, I am surprised at your
admiration for me, / for dear you are my root.*

—Hafiz

1980, London

(The mirror, in Urdu poetry, is the reflections of the heart, among many other motifs, says Auntie Nuzhat, as poetic Urdu vocabulary comes back to me from childhood's lessons.)

The moon, in my reflection, keep changing postures
In pain, see how it twists its shape.

In my lonely place I reside sometimes—
The moon, a mist, a fog at times

Hiding its resplendent face, as if ashamed to love,
Among the darkness that surrounds it

The bird looks at the moon, grounded on earth still,
Moon on the skies looks beyond, hungry for love

Downing itself, drowning, then drooping,
Rising daily, surviving daily, daily dying for love—

The moon in the mirror changes angles so quickly.

Azmaish Examination

Then there will be the Companions of the
Right Hand...and those foremost in Faith
will be foremost in the Hereafter. These will be
those Nearest to Allah in the Gardens of Bliss:
A number of people from those of old, and
a few from those of later times. They will be
on Thrones encrusted with gold and precious
stones, reclining on them, facing each other.
—Sura 56, "The Inevitable Event

2002, London

Why sorrow over time when we can understand *time's voice?*
    Time, a drop of essence;
    River, a drop on earth's hemisphere
Time is a desert and garden too
    Time, a softness, a hard rock too
    A waterfall time is, a frozen lake too
    So why does time flows so fast
    Even when we don't want it to?
    Don't accuse time so much, O accuser
    Do you even see what *your purpose might be?*
Your eternal sadness, that completion
    Couldn't find you—time, don't make it your enemy
    Rather, think of time as *pain's healing balm*
    When time is seen for what it really is.

Grieve for sorrows? Why do you?
    Listen deeply to the voice of pain soothing,
    Not wounding, you
For your heart's salvation.
    For time has always been your friend.
    [Amazing, Nuzhat Auntie. Ameen.]

In the Desert, a Metropolis Rose

*No nation can rise to the height of glory unless
your women are side by side with you.*
—Baba-i-Qaum; Muhammad Ali Jinnah

August 15, 2021

This was my toughest piece to translate thus far. Uncle Faiz
helped me with understanding Auntie Nuzhat's complex Urdu dic-
tion and multicultural word combinations. Auntie Nuzhat has several pieces in this book that have various nuances of the desert motif,
based on distinct experiences and historical observations. Her poems
remind me that each piece of art has many perspectives, depending
on one's work, job efforts, or home nurturing consciousness.

Many congratulations to one and all
In celebrating the land we claimed to love,
This place where the devoted one spoke of unity,
Faith, and love for everyone,
But say, why leave now?
And what's happened to that nation made for the pure
In spirit and body, whose hard works were meant for one and
    all?
Some leave for the Middle East.
Some leave for the West,
Calling out dreams for that land
That first gave their candles a flame,
A spark from which to rise for justice,
Bent toward peace for everyone.

Now other people pray for that same homeland
From far, far away, remembering what it was built on.

Have you travelers forgotten your
Homeland's people, whose evil eyes
Kept gazing on what others have,
Given by the same God?
That dream we saw of the nation's glowing
Rays have shattered, haven't they?
Where time has brought more justice and peace
In other lands where those values we esteem
Are practiced much, much more than
Where we left—from where we once belonged?
But time shall come, as Quaid-e-Azam said,
When *good works become consistent with our love*

For each on land or sea as those who went away,
Praying more each day for people's independence
So that each may walk with head held high,
Appreciating the lands they've still to build

Instead of corrupting the order painted freely
By those who soar through inner struggles—
This *Jihad e zindage*, struggle of life,
Conquering our own tribulations and temptations,
Not finding faults with others, nor grabbing what others
Own, nor casting out people in vain.

Each dawn, the morning's beauty comes to me
Through tears I've shed, reminding me of the land's once
Fragrant breeze, where I, too, struggled as traveling minority,
Entrapped once as in a cage till pure breezes, sorrow-laden,
Came back to me... Someday we all shall walk on that pure

Land, head held high, hoping for humanity's independence
From corrupting ways that hold love back from land's blessedness.

Aeena Kiyoon Na Doon
Kae Tamashaa Kaheen Jisay
The Outlandish Scenes of
Brouhaha that the Mirror Shows

Auntie Nuzhat's short dramatic script performed in front of seven
hundred people several years ago among other creative pieces

Recorded on August 22, 2021

This piece has a certain urgency and speaks to that waning
group of people in any community that intended to hold on to good
traditions while drowning in the sea of being lost from either community. So many families come to new lands for hard work and the
love of riches but have a rough time maintaining their wise, ancient
codes or moral traditions while trying to blend in with the popular
cultures.

Auntie Nuzhat's short, dramatic scene speaks volumes to people who seem to have made it in America but have lost the essential
values of their ethnic and religious identities. From another point
of view, that is the point of full assimilation instead of accultura-
tion—the healthy eighties version of win-win in both or tricultural
experiences.

In New York's most posh area, the Neazi family are sitting
around. The missus looks worried. Mr. Neazi is uninvolved in his

wife's anxious mentality. He is looking at the newspaper—maybe reading, maybe not.

"How long will you be reading that paper?" she says as if wanting some of his attention.

Daddi Amma comes into the room from another room. She has a sixth sense—that mother's intuition that many are losing now—and knows everything that seems to be happening in the room and well beyond.

"Why give *excess freedom* to the young girls these days? *This is America.* You know all the things that can happen, and I don't have to list them," she says.

Mr. Neazi says, "We can't take kids and place them safely in one room as treasures. They need to discover the places, who they are, and where they are."

Mrs. Neazi looks at the window. What kind of dark evening is this? It is a remnant of her foreboding—big, gray clouds everywhere.

Mr. Neazi comes closer to her and says, "Don't worry, my dear, the girls shall be coming soon. Even this storm will subside soon."

One more hour passes. They imagine they are not waiting up for the girls.

The girls' voices are finally heard in the distance—the carefree echolalia—and they hear them coming in, laughing, gaily, perhaps burdened but still gaily.

"I tell you, really, Sarah, Brian did not want me to leave this early. He wanted me to dance with him. I guess I can't imagine who else there could be for me, you know?"

"How can you tell Mummy?" says Ayesha. Still not finished, Ayesha adds, "How could you even do that or think of doing such a careless thing?"

Mr. Neazi just listens to something in the background as if he is in his own world, but Daddi Amma seems to hear things even when she is not there in the living room.

"*Oh, Jesus Christ!*" the careless daughter says out loud! "*Why are you guys still up?*" Sarah seems to think it's only the crazy, fanatic parents who are always still up, waiting for the return of the children who all grown up and supposedly mature.

273

As if reading her mind, Mummy says, "Do you not understand that your parents are still up? You know that your dad had heart surgery a while ago, and your mom has high blood pressure! Where were you all this time?"

Mrs. Neazi mumbles something as if realizing, *Something great has been lost here.*

Don't think that these are the only ones here who seem to have gotten lost. Nothing is lost with blending with people, but to completely give oneself away and lose one's manners and honor—these are more essential than our lives.

(The audience wonders which parent makes such an assertion. When insensible things happen, both parents seem to blend in together into a parental blob.)

Sarah and Ayesha, like criminals, are bending their heads in front of their mother, tears in their eyes, knowing have been *transgressing limits of protocols on how to behave properly.* Sarah had promised something to that Brian, and she is going to become a mother (without even a marriage contract or God's approval).

"*It is all too late now,*" says the voice of the room. "*Too late. Too late for all that.*"

Maybe it was Ayesha's voice. Maybe it was their guilt saying so. But clearly, their values were getting mixed up with the outside values that seemed not to care about anything but lust, parties, etc. There is nothing wrong with outside values; the only thing wrong is not having one's traditions and God-given protocols.

Sarah would come from school, and only the babysitter's face would be in view as if there were no parents to watch over them, to guide them, no one but a babysitter as substitute parent.

Now the parents acted as if they had already given the necessary values of the family's traditions. But they had been too busy in their lives for family life and too busy for God.

Ayesha's upbringing: Ayesha says, "Our traditions had come from the maid, not from our parents."

Sarah is now following those traditions.

Ayesha, who still has a voice, says this to her mother, who seems shocked: "*We would not stand like criminals* in front of you, had you given us more wisdom of our values. Who were we supposed to be?" she asks.

"I'm sorry, Mummy, *but we are moving out. It is too late now.*"

"I've given myself to Brian," says Sarah with no respect whatsoever.

Ayesha looks on.

Mr. Neazi comes closer to his wife (as if he had been there for her all along).

"*Why did we work so hard?*" he says to a family, who he thinks is listening. "So that you would have no troubles in this world. Why did we work too hard in this land, in this country? For you all!"

"Beti, I had raised you like gentle flowers...not to be torn apart before your time," says Mr. Neazi.

Like stone, Sarah looks askance.

"*But it's too late now,*" mourns Mr. Neazi, as if finally joining in Mrs. Neazi's life anxiety now. He suddenly holds her tightly, but she sits with her hands on her face and cries as if there is no more tomorrow.

Mr. Neazi sits next to her on the plush sofa and says nothing. One can hear his tears in the background run through her sobbing.

Daddi Ammi looks on from the distance as if nothing else needs to be said.

January 17, 2022

I suppose this is a *mushada*—an observatory of experiences—not really a full personal experience nor even my story but the story of all those who became enamored with their ways of lives and desires and forgot about a few essentials. Such is life these days. I have witnessed these scenes again and again in my traveling memory, which comes back to sit in the present moment as I make myself think of all the women who loved being moms, whose children somewhere borrowed them back, and moms who flew back to their origins.

Perhaps you, too, reader dear, have noticed such observatories of experiences…

Zara

For our dear Zara (from Nani Ammi and Nanu)

A rosebud is she, Zara,
Our floret Angelique
From morn's dew has she come
From heart's gardens has she

Balmy light to our eyes
Heart's affirming delight
Friend to Maya
Sister's sheen light

Lovely Guriya, intelligent is she
From Navaid and Anita,
Nanu, Nani, Dadda, Daddi's
Darling moonbeam

Our strength to lean on
Uncle's light, Uncle's *noor* is she
Zara Guriya, lovelier than the moon,
Our rosebud is she

In a Quaint, Tiny Town

A Raghastan existed—
A small seed of persons
Began growing that town
From flat expanse of desert
To something bearing fruit

It was a hope turned into a dream,
Turning back into hopes again
As the land blossomed,
So did its people, little by little,
Breezes blowing softly, freely

Some ask, "What's happening to *that nation?*"
Others say togetherness is there, reviving her;
The more divided its people have gotten,
Some are striving as others gave up,
Same as deserted towns lying bare.

Geet of the Masoom Era
Childhood Sojourning

Aao Sajnee, hum tm khalay,
Kail kay ji bhalanyen—tum bano khusboo; hum bano yar
Tum bano kinara (beach); hum banay sagaar (seaside)
Sagaar—Samundaar
Tum taak ayenn
Laut kaar phir hum jaean
Tum bano dhoop; hum banqy sayaaa;
Dhoop say milnay sayaaa ayaaa,
Phir bhi mil na payaay
Aao sajnee, hum tum khalaeen, kael kay ji bahlaayeen
Tum bano Ganga/Hum bane Jamna
Ekhi Sangaam paar aa milaayn hum, phir kho jaieeen
Tum Bano Sajnee
Aao Sajnee, hum tum khalay
Phir bhi na tum go payeen-
Aao sajnee hum tum khalayen; khael kay ji bahlayeen;
Tum Bano chandaa; hum bane chakori;
Tum say khalleen; khael ke ji bahlayeen;

Come, O friend of childhood days,
Let us play till we thrive again
You be the beach; I play the seaside
To you I run back from those childhood's playgrounds
Returning still, we go back to the origin—
You, the fragrance long gone;
I, the perfect dream child's friend

Two childhood friends of purity meet,
Forever playing since young days—the innocence of those days
Come, childhood's friend, come play like those old days
Let's play until our senses thrive,
Still never to meet again
Like two different seas that touch but never meet
Childhood is a place of mind's retreating
Two childhood friends of purity meet, keep meeting
Still, they played when little—the innocence of those days
Shade came to meet the sunshine; still, they never met again
Since those old childhood days, still subsiding, still retreating
You be the Ganges; I, the Jamna
Meeting in the same juncture where only
childhood meetings happen

Imaginatively, the two childhood friends are drifting back to childhood for a time. There is no other purer friendship but the ones of complete honesty and purity of souls/spirits that God destines in people of His choosing.

Vignettes for Thought

San Antonio, Texas
On June 20, 2022

Contents

1. The Russian Gentleman who remembered his Grandma 285
2. Penmanship Pointillism...288
3. Munna Dada and my Trip to Pakistan................................292
4. The Grand-Sweet Lady from Whiting New Jersey 296
5. That Sufi Monk and Earthly Rose 300

The Russian Gentleman who remembered his Grandma

The Russian gentleman had left Mother
Russia for Rova Farms, New Jersey.

The gentleman did not want to tell the whole story back then in the eighties as I went to have a nice Russian breakfast with my father who loved all people. Olga, his wife from another culture, and Ogloo, were a strange combination of people, even from a nine year old's eyes.

As we breakfasted on the world's most perfectly square grilled potatoes and the thickest omelet with a thicker pancake and syrup, tears fell from Ogloo's eyes as he joined us while managing the blue and white restaurant filled with people from everywhere in the Garden State.

Since then, I had met many Russians or Soviets, not as many Ukrainians, but many Russians, including a beautiful blonde boss of mine from a College town. She and I taught and loved much Russian literature in a certain Illinois campus way back when, and it sure is refreshing to make healthy connection with one's boss as it is with regular literary friends. But I digress.

Baba Ogloo stared into a vacant space as if her were looking upon the faces of his ancestors with betrayal. After all, in the eighties, everyone thought, whoever went as far as the USA, that s (he) was finding the perfect sense of new-found freedom. It was freedom for me, and many others, as kids who lived happily in our during as much as in our past. Freedom itself was enduring—more than any commodity on earth, said Baba Ogloo, as he ate his chunk of his wife-made omelet with us, knowing that my father listened to every word.

His wife joined us with her chef's apparel and a pretty German dress that looked like a gown that my aunt would wear.

"He feels guilty even now, that's what it is," she said with a ladle in her right hand.

"Guilty?" "For making oneself happy in the land of the free," said my dad.

"When you know that your ancestors and maybe your own father may not approve of surreptitious landmarks from one powerful land to another that only has superficial similitudes, then you will always carry the burden of feeling betrayed by your own ego towards those who gave us everything, even hearty approval for marrying Olga."

Silence prevailed between the syrup and the pancakes delving into our hungry mouths as Olga and Ogloo held hands. She went back to the kitchen—as he told us stories of his boyhood in Moscow.

To be a Muscovite, he said, *one only needs to keep a few secrets from the government*: like one's complete Faith in a Higher Power than their own Reds.

How's that, Dad asked. Won't they know if you're privately worshiping your Higher Power?

I don't understand, I said, though was just a kid.

See, when you grow up reading Dostoyevsky, you learn early on that man is capable of both good and wicked deeds, pure faith and pure corruption, pure truth and pure lies—and people like Raskolnikov are more common than you think—finding new and sick ways to kill off one's landlord's wife or female innkeeper, whichever case it may be out of injuries to the head at birth or such.

I know that book well enough, said my father, who also had read much Russian fiction known the world over for its humanistic grieving. Do schools teach Dostoyevsky much in Moscow?

Not if they can help it. But good teachers, as in anywhere else, find ways of squeezing him into the curriculum just as good Italian teachers squeeze in a little Boccaccio before the daily catechisms made mandatory by the church senate—why? So, the kids would get a little freedom in thinking about right and wrong choices from a secular lens. If I didn't have my grandmother looking about me when my mum and dad went working like good old peasants day in and day out, I might have become a Raskolnikov himself, said Ogloo.

Such conversations went on and on and as I ate from the Russian pancakes filled with sugary toppings and loads of butter, sometimes taking a sip now and then, of my dad's coffee, which he insisted was too bitter for me.

Years later, my dad and I took time off from a great family gathering to attend to the funeral of the locally famous Brother Ogloo. My dad had an intuition that his Rova Farms friend was dying and came to see him just before death. We were served tea by his loving wife with tears in her eyes—served with love on Russian tea trays, red and gold and silver. I'll never forget those fragile Russian tea cups as the human heart is as fragile like fine glass.

When we went to his bedside, all of his eight children, all born in America, were there, standing or kneeling, making prayers for their father, the man who said he could have been a Raskolnikov, were in not for the embracing of his grandmother when his very busy parents went to work day in, day out.

"My friend. You are here, too, for me. How did you know," said he in his newly acquired masterful English.

"I had a feeling deep in my gut that you were going, my brother, to someplace better than here," said my dad with much moisture in his eyes. He kissed Baba Ogloo's temple, and the sons grabbed his arms.

"*We all sense the going of a good man,*" said another guest of honor. "When a good man goes, all the family and as many true ones are by his side."

"*He has made peace with everyone he could,*" said his gracious wife, giving me a tight hug, as if she just saw me yesterday, eating her Russian pancakes with extra honey on top.

Penmanship Pointillism

She was on the liberal side of conservatism when I first met her—don't know how many years ago—the dust scatters from my memory.

I tended to have friends who were ten or more years older than me while most people my age were seeking friends their age or much younger than me. Maybe it was another Dad trait that I had inherited, though I was the louder version of my dad in many respects of daily life. His laughter, however, could shake a room, and *he'd never laugh at people, only with them at universal frailties, instinctively.*

The first time I went to her home she was taking care of her ailing mother, a quite unpopular thing to do nowadays. Her mom was rocking on that rocking chair enjoying giving small commands that sounded like requests to her doting daughter. That rocking chair never creaked while I was there, nor did my friend at the requests of her mother—from another tea request to yet another jam on a slice of bread. A variety of cute animals were everywhere in the surroundings, but I would notice the bluebird and all its cousin birds would fly into this friend's yard, *choosing her yard of bird furnishings over other neighbors' fancier, greener yards* that were more austere and foreboding for heavenly birds to want to enter. Bird-eye view of mere man rests on the fact that creatures love the poised rich with cold tendencies; Birds' view of men, however, seem that they love the nourishing of heart, though they may seem cold from the outside, distant to those of greener, more austere yards cultivated by hired gardeners' hands.

I would hear my grandmother's voice saying, "You know the right people to pick as your friend," not those tribal types who stick to their own feather until the feathers get bloodied by a wayfarer with bad intentions.

Instinct and intuition, in this friend, too, was cultivated from within the forte of her Norwegian home that relished good manners but *virtuous manners to all of creation, not just her tribe from superficial ways.* This is probably why the bluebird and all its cousins would, in turn, relish landing for a bird break in her yard, eating of her bread crumbs and other furnishings of God's great sustenance.

This friend, as true friend's mirror one's inner conscience, did not possess the look of any certain religion on her face, nor did I— both could be from anywhere at any given time from any era. One need not try and possess religion as one possesses a demon with great desire or demolition of one's other aspects of the self.

Selfhood comes in many layers, as birds know, too, flying high in happy spirt, aligning themselves with their small yet larger purposes back to the heavenly realms from which they emerged. It's only the clingy ones of earth who much find Darwinian connections to larger lizards that God made extinct for His own purposes, by the little hands of men.

When the tides of political tsunami changed abruptly, the birds' choices of which homes to land on did not change, nor did the calming balm temperament of my friend, whose religious institution did not stonewall her into a higher pedestal of her own making. Even the great Teacher sent to the lost sheep of Israel, some of whom remain lost, of their own choosing, said clearly, "Do not call me good, for only God is good."

If he did not place himself in any man-made pedestal, why should those who love and revere his teachings in diverse ways try to do pedestal building on themselves, later worshiping themselves, while claiming to worship the One who created them? In caring for her mother, this friend was doing what any servant of God might do: care for people who are loving but not always in love with caring for us in return. Caring for our loved ones does not require a return as the birds that come feed happily on our lawns do not require a thank you card.

Today, this friend has not changed. Time's war on the elderly has not changed her attitude on serenity, the inner kind that does not bother who says what about whom to whom and why.

She is not of the world, as I am not of the world all the time, but in the world for my ordained time, however long, and by whichever route of suffering or joy the Blessed Maker has planned—while human hands plan all kinds of tickets to salvation with a greedy gut intention, thinking that we must know whether we will be damned or saved.

Truth is, *no one knows who is hell-bound and who is Heaven-bound, for both tickets must be earned*; even birds of any feather know instinctively that they have a choice which yard to eat from, and which prettier seeming yard to ignore, for their larger blessings back to the skies from which they emerged.

I celebrate all the people, along with my friend who gladly took care of her mom while her rocker never creaked, whose choices were aligned with their works, whose every bread crumb was chosen by themselves, or when given, they took graciously, thankfully, knowing that their placement on life's map never really mattered; it was only what they did with what they had that would let them fly freely from the inside looking out. To fly with heavy hearts and deeply engraved sins—*not everybody has to have a hundred sins—must be the poorest way to go anywhere.*

One time, early morn, when I went walking with this brisk walker friend, me in my heavy load of sadness engulfing my once-light spirited moves, she, in her brisk calisthenics in the midst of her youthful ambling, a very stiff-necked man from another side of the street came nearer and nearer us with his a friendlier, fluffier dog than anything that he seemed to be. When we ladies smiled at the dog in friendly way, the dog responded with a smiley guffaw, trying to come near us from the spaces within the street.

Then came a surprising comment from the blustering mule of a man, for no earthly reason but inner rage and angst from some place inside him that must deeply haunt him from his relationships to female humans:

"Why, why are you two women stalking me," said he, (as if any woman of sense would ever come near that raging, grumbling man).

"We are not stalking you," said one of us, I cannot remember which one.

The other one of us petted the dog lightly to appease the disoriented dog more than the disoriented man. Then, "Have a nice one," said another one of us, feeling sympathy for the man in the beginning of his raging remark, that later turned into a bitter feeling of why would he say a thing like that.

A few dinners ago, a cousin of mine, wiser than the times said, sometimes we just take the abuses of raging people for a little while without saying a word because we don't know what storms are brewing up inside their chaotic minds.

I never forgot that incident of two of us calming people who loved peace and quiet and nature and God, with a brouhaha of man who wanted to communicate something, but could only get something disruptive out of himself.

To this day, since my wise cousin's remark about taking in some small abuses for the greater good, I tend to do this, and find that wild dogs are masculine in their frenzied natures than actual pets and bird visitors that come by for their temporal appeasement.

I hope that strange man we saw on that road on an early morning walk finds something greater than his wild temper to live for—and that small birds may someday visit his furnished yard.

Munna Dada and my Trip to Pakistan

My daughter, very proud to be an American, even right now, tries to remind me every once in a while, "We didn't come here like normal immigrants with one suitcase and big dreams. Why do you act like such an immigrant when you're so New Jersey?"

As if being "so New Jersey" is an exotic perfume that wards of the droppings of New York; that is undiscovered beauty of the Garden State, (which does have undiscovered beauty, even near the wooded Jersey Devil forests, infamous for their mythologies). So, I tell her if I'm not an immigrant's daughter, then nobody is an immigrant's daughter or granddaughter, for I'm the average immigrant's daughter that always wanted to make her parents happy and proud of my choices in life. I loved being from New Jersey via Chicago, (where my father landed, not a normal thing for most people emigrating permanently elsewhere), via Lahore, Pakistan, via Bihar, India, via all the Semitic lands from which my grandfathers and grandmothers settled themselves down in the Subcontinent, some of the mixing with the locals of the Indian continent, vast in her democratic fusing of creeds and traditions.

What I supposed I loved most about being from New Jersey was the freedom I enjoyed in my schooling with freedom-loving teachers who said exactly what they wanted, regardless of extra-care politeness that politicians use to their advantage that sometimes becomes a disadvantage. I loved the bluntness of New Jersey attitudes that we wear on our sleeves as we wear our hearts of our sleeves, so to speak: If ones dislikes something, it is said upfront, no flowers or apple pies sweetening the atmosphere until it seems time to stick a knife in someone's back. If one hates an ideology or what people do with an ideology, we New Jersey-trained people say, we hate it, and we mean it, until we are proved differently. In other places, you are adored until the mobs say differently, while beguiling you with apple pies and sweets.

So, with the political turmoil that had nothing to do with my interests or, lack of interest in deceiving politics of the day, I forced myself to go back to the emotional/affective clime of my motherland, the original one that accepts all people's inner diversity as well as outer diversity. I forced myself to begin trying to wear more modest clothing—the elegant hijab that I tried out with passion for Allah for nine months—made my daughters shun me all of a sudden, and perhaps I wasn't as strong in my faith—or, maybe I was in my interiority, but needed my daughters' attentions as "the mom they used to know," (vibrant, cheerful most of the time, eager-to-please, vivacious and carefree towards everyone, while minding my manners and my Faith expectations, (still).

In any case, parts of me misses that aspect of the me I used to know, and cries that I do not understand my own transformation towards a more sorrowful person, (still peaceful and kind most of the time, but perturbed by society's downfall and the previous school's interference in my personal ways)—parts of cries quietly in the bathroom and shower after having taken care of my husband's bath, and wonders what Allah expects of my with so many tribulations at once and why. I try not to question everything, for I am no Iqbal who did question everything in his collections; however, once in a while I do feel somewhat dissociated from the Kausam I used to know, (as if parts my being were eaten up by demons and thrown in the garbage of an immigrant-hating realm). Still, Allah has been so benevolent to send his beautiful creatures, redbirds, along my path, along my windowsill in the most impromptu occasions. I know that I am Allah's and that He will never be cruel to me for I can handle what comes my way for His sake alone.

What a digression from what I intended to say about Munna Dada in Pakistan whom we sisters met only once. I do not know if my sisters remember him or that special moment of his magnanimity inside his poverty, but I do. And I cry remembering that such people have existed in the vicissitudes of our family.

Munna Dada, the unlettered brother from all the super-educated brothers of his family was the youngest of the five brothers from Darbhanga, Bihar, India where my own grandfather was Chief of Police in the daytime and popular poet in the nighttime when many visitors would sit on the poetry floor near him as he and fellow poets had Hal-Qal, a "high" in reading poems with a singers' flair while smoking tobacco.

Munna Dada, though he was not educated as all the other brothers—engineers, principal, police officer, teacher, and postal service officer—*chose to be a caretaker of the family.* He did not marry a class, well-off wife, but a poor lady from a noble family; however, he his wife with all his heart. He had a special education son that he also cared for, (In the Pakistan of the eighties when I visited, special education students were not attended to very well as they are in the United States); Munna Dada had his hands and mind full with things to do in a day. Sometimes, he even helped his wife make chapattis and parathas—breads made on flat irons or tandoors in their small, bare kitchen, hardly walkable. For a poor man in a patriarchal nation, (hate to say this, but it is true), he was the ultimate feminist, as was my grandfather, always believing in what women and the underprivileged in society could potentially do.

In their tiny living room was a bed in the corner where the special education boy slept, and a sofa where his guest were served hot chai and desserts. When my sisters and I were "made" to visit him by my mother—for all elders are to be respected—was her motto—Munna Dada not only treated us as though he had known us all along, but he had Pakistani *shalwar qamizzes* made for us with the exact measurements his wife took, and the dresses were ready that same day for a tailor lived nearby. Mine was starry with a sky-blue shading; my middle sister's was pink with similar starry patterns; and my youngest sister's outfit was bright red, like her sobriquet, "Lali."

"He must have spent his entire week's salary for those outfits," said my mother, after we left the tiny house in which they laughed, smiled, and shared their joys with us. We wondered how people could be so happy and have almost nothing at all compared to how comfortably we middle class Americans lived our life in New Jersey.

Gratitude for what one has, whether material wealth or familial wealth, allows one to be closer to Allah goes the motto, and why wouldn't the Creator of Benevolence give one more if we were grateful, not scornful for who and what we have accompanying us in this earthly journey? Yet the opposite happens in wealthy societies too often, the spoiled, upper echelons of Pakistani society also: *the more one has, the more one scorns who and what one has in life*, thereby producing a society of ungrateful people scorning themselves and one another. Munna Dada taught us a simple lesson just by being himself: It is God who chooses one's destiny; yet, it is man that must work as caretakers of any destiny to find happiness in that journey.

"When you have Faith and Good Works for Allah, you can live on anything," said my mother, (whose own life was going to be shortened by eleven years due to an impromptu onset of dementia right after the wrong doctor put too much anesthesia in her system for too long a time for a simple woman's surgical procedure. But I shall always remember Munna Dada, the most humble Pakistani and family man that I met, feeling as if I had known my grandfather's younger brother all along. Surely, I remember each saying of my mother who would analyze the good actions of each person that we met together.

The Grand-Sweet Lady from Whiting New Jersey

*Sura Zumar, The Crowds: "**Those who listen to the Word**, and **follow the best (meaning)** in it: Those are the ones whom Allah has guided, and those are the ones endued with understanding…it is for those who fear their Lord, that lofty mansions, one above another, have been built: beneath them flow rivers of delight: such is the Promise of Allah: Never doth Allah fail in (His) promise." 39:18–20.*

You may have seen this lady somewhere, a grand Italian lady, much like the paintings of the Renaissance (Italian-style), who goes anywhere she wants yet maintains a certain flair and fleur des lis about her. You will want to meet her, perhaps take a picture with her, but she will not be ostentatious, nor will she find ways to make enemies with people, unless defending her familial way of life.

She had peculiar habits when her husband met her at a dinner party—in parts of New Jersey, it is still customary to meet future partners in life at dinner parties, not on-line dating that grand women do not do, nor cheap housing that incorporates a place without God in the picture.

Do people like that still exist, you might ask. She was from Canada via her parents' travels. But after her parents were done with the beauties and luxuries of costly living in biodiverse Canada, she found herself going back to Whiting, New Jersey where anyone *could say anything that came to the lips, genuine, sincere, or callous sometimes,* without being bombarded with questions or hate mail.

Vanessa Bernadette Castiglione, possibly descended from the Italian diplomat, but her family wouldn't tell you that—did have four children of that good marriage to Bernardo, the Italian and the

Jew from both sides of his family. The young boy she liked some-what in her high school prom, the only person she thought she liked, turned out to be exactly what she did not like: pompous, belittling women, self-malignant, and inclined to violence. When she said No!—for the fourteenth time, the pompous brat finally left and found a Princeton-trained corrupted female of the same ilk; as God has explained in various Suras and perhaps, Revelations before that, the people of like mentality tend to be near people of like mentality, especially if they choose corruption over decent venues of life. It is not always the case, however, and eventually, everyone, I believe, has a chance to meet like mentalities over the popular understanding that "opposites attract." This was not so in Vanessa's case, nor in her mother's, nor in her grandmother's—they "came from a long line of love," as the country song goes.

Vanessa prayed every day and did her vespers and matins as well as in-between prayers, so that she felt deeply about her direct com-munication faculties with God Almighty, while being in the world as much as she could, metaphorically.

Anyway, Bernardo and Vanessa finally learned each other's foi-bles, a good part of a historical lesson in any marriage or book. When they were good, they were very, very good, as the limerick goes, but when they were mean, they were horrid to each other—that is, when prayers became like formulas in their hearts, as children are some-times taught to write in formulaic patterns, which do not end up doing them any favors spiritually, emotionally, or in psychic resil-ience means, as most good instructors know.

Not being diplomatic like her grand grand-grand relative, the original Castiglione, known for his marvelous answers and chivalric actions with expecting anything from anyone, Vanessa insisted that Bernardo have no say in the selection of their children's names!

"How dare you dishonor my side of the family," said her beloved who had changed over the years somewhat, and had begun wonder-ing about his man-powers in the family he thought was ruled equally when they first met through that memorable family dinner when he instantly asked her that question, and she instantly responded as if her were the only person out of 500 dinner guests in the room.

"I dare because we women carry the children in our wombs," and because it is high time that feminists undo the damages that have been done to us women.

"So, let me understand the logic here?" "*You're saying that one family, our family will be taking the entire burden of feminism onto our family's terrain, and that I am to blame* for all of men's shortcomings over the centuries of patronizing patriarchy?"

"That is what I'm saying, my love, my heart."

He became as silent as a dervish monk, my cousin's term for handling most unexpected family crises.

Bernardo, being a feminist anyway, as much as his long line of educated, sensible people of New Jersey from educated sensible Jews and Italians who had no problems with each other, reminded her of her own grand-grand-grand ancestor—but she could not face that her husband could be grander than she was, for she had begun changing into some selfish patterns when she gave up her vespers and matins or, her deeper connection to the Lord of Creation, which most pragmatic elites in her groups had also stopped concerning themselves over.

Long story short, her children did have blessings—bendiciones as her Puerto Rican friend, Julia, would say about family and children.

Vanessa, after five years of marriage, had named one after another salad dressing names: Dijon was her first son. Honey was her second daughter. Caesar was the third son. And, when she ran out of ideas and got post-partum depression about her fading good looks, she called the fourth one, Bonaparte—(who, like his name, did part nicely, but part he did, from the rest of the family nest.

The salad dressing children formed a curious bond of taking care of each other when the mother and father had gone too much into their ostrich selves, forgetting that children's sacred lives could not be neglected like salad dressing.

Dijon opened up the finest restaurant business that his savings after college loans and grandfather's generosity could find him.

He invited sweetly his sister, Honey, and brother, Caesar to join him in this family business for each of them were excellent chefs who used good, pure ingredients according to ethical histories of what makes fine ingredients. No blood sausage. No hunting meat taken by the neck or by strangling. No pork products, though they did lose some money for many customers missed that element in the menu.

The parents began waking up to this scene of genuine camaraderie between siblings in the ways that countries should make up for their cruelties upon each other.

They looked into the marital mirror to find inner joys that they had buried. They hugged once again, and kissed once again, and knew that names had made a difference. Where was Bonaparte, however, making his fortune? No one knew yet.

A motto began going around about the ***Fine Salads Restaurant in New Jersey***: Salads are our main meals; pizzas and pastas, our sides.

People of health loved that idea, and throngs of people who enjoyed good food, great décor, fine company, and Godly attitudes would surround that restaurant. Their lines were much like Mother Russia handing out breads to hundreds and thousands-seeming at a time, except it was the opposite with them—people came from ways off to attend Fine Salads where salads were indeed the main themes, hundreds of varieties of salads.

Bernardo looked at his wife *with a different kind of smile*, other than sardonic, other than feminist, other than scornful. With appreciation—that the one he trusted to make a marriage work made his marriage better than he had seen among his friends.

That Sufi Monk

Sura Ma'iada, The Table Spread—5:3: "And let not the hatred of some people in shutting you out of the Sacred Mosque lead you to transgression and hostility on your part. Help yet one another in righteousness and piety, but help ye not one another in sin and rancor."

I have met thousands of loud, rambunctious people, fun in extroverted ways. Other times, I have just met loud people. Often, I am told by those who may not know me that I am a rather loud person, too. Whether this is mostly true, or mostly false is irrelevant, but envisioning the quietest of persons, one trains oneself to be quieter than one normally is on any given day.

We all have trouble understanding ourselves and why we function the way we do at some key point in our lives. For some of us, music helps us make those connections deeper. For others, it is art, and still others, hobbies of building things or people up, or building people down. Still others find self-understanding through the culinary arts, dancing, exercising, or through motivational talks, or selling healthy items or dogma on which they believe. Still others find joy in self-understanding through archeological trips or, tripping through the archeology of language, as one favorite professor (parent) of mine.

Not one of these hobbies seem better or worse than another— for each person has a forte and a flair somewhere hidden away that comes back in crises times particularly. What is good for one person may not be good for another person, depending on one's interiority and emotional makeup—also depending on how perilous a concept or art is for that individual. After all, good can be done with many proclivities, and so can evil as well as waste of time and energy for others.

As I sit here on this large, obscure rock that still hurts the lower crevices of my back during this trip, I look out at the wide sea—ebullient and edgy as we humans tend to be when misery and joy turn their tides into us, peering into our soul's abyss. In the dream, there was a boat and purple shadows—but that boat was not meant for me. It reminded me of a place that people go to when they're not fully aware of themselves, a kind of internal purgatorial space floating down some memory lane only, forgetting to move forward with their sacred spaces inside. When we are busy liking this, disliking that, loving this, obsessing over that, hating this, and loathing that—all aspects of changing human nature, we end up, perhaps, missing the larger pictures of our lives. Even in the state of disliking anything or any habits within societies, it is a happier-causing state to treat all people to how we wish to be treated, to exchange civil discourses in genuine ways of appreciation and silence, as my own devout Christian neighbors did today and yesterday, without expecting anything in return. I wondered how fast anyone could arrive, (as requested), at any crisis scene in quiet, composed demeanor, while getting the first response needed in minutes. This practical reality of stoic good works was indeed the opposite of the chaotic city dream about young kids forgetting to know their various functions in their stressed lives.

Many young children, in this dream, were playing with large, ceramic toys made in human and animal imagery, lost children, lost from their parents and grandparents' cares—making noises in the summer, wondering where they are supposed to go, and what their purposes are in this life in their stages of life. They tried to guide other children, but each group kept getting lost in the busy city of toys and more toys—it was I who was handicapped in the dream, but I had an idea of where I needed to go in the city. The wheelchair pushed itself amid the mayhem of the large toys, crowds of children bored with their duties, and honking cars going in many directions. In a noisy world, one could try and be quiet—many other philosophies are all about shouting until we are heard somewhere in the world, until we are shining bright and threatening in a city that is awake sleeping. As the dream ended, I was back on the rock looking out at the sea view as layers of waves moved to their own rhythm.

The Sufi Monk whom we met in our earlier journey is much like this: a paradox among the extroverted ones in each crowd of fun-loving, jocose people. I first met the Sufi Monk, an old-school Dervish of contemporary upbringing when I was twelve or so. He arrived in a stylish simplicity with the Rose of Earthly Roses—(For us Muslims and Catholics, The Blessed Virgin Mary, on whom be peace, is the traditional spiritual Rose, as in the case of Jean de Meun's Roman de la Rose). But the Rose of Earthly Roses never left the side of Sufi Monk—Dervishes do not need to take any oath of celibacy, for marriage could be an equally spiritual experience, if one allows it to be.

"Mom, Sufi Monk and Earthly Rose left their scarf…their watch…their jacket…something," each time they'd visit us from their travels. "Do we send these things back to them?"

"Not at all. They'll be back Insha'Allah," Mom would say. Insha'Allah ensured that every decision was left to the Highest Force possible—Allah—with a hint of optimism with reality's acceptance.

I did not know then, that Sufi Monk and Earthly Rose would become huge parts of our lives in all moments of crises as well as happier times.

"Maybe it's a sign that they are going to be part of your later life, too," Mom said. Mom was like that. *She'd say things out of pure intuition that would come true when we least expected them to.* Earthly Rose also said things out of the intuitive blues that would eventually happen. But they'd always add, Insha-Allah, with a meaningful smile after hours of quiet worship though talking was part of their functions in any gathering.

Decades later, I noticed in every gathering that people would speak volumes of interesting family history, or world history, light politics, or light poetics, or even scientific discoveries—but Sufi Monk *mostly listened*, while having the quiet audacity to put all the dishes away, (that even the most helpful women in gatherings forgot to do), even placing heavy items in the dishwasher, as if he hadn't any resources that might help him with most menial of chores. After making chai for dozens of visitors, Sufi Monk continued listening eagerly, offering occasional therapeutic thoughts to ponder. Genuinely he would listen, as people continued sharing large ideas that occurred spontaneously in the ways the late Victorians discussed the ongoing of their era: cheerful, sagacious, and suave. But not Sufi Monk. He'd join in the laughter that was generalized, *never at anyone*, but thoughtful, vociferous laughter, pliable pauses, and still people wondered why Earthly Rose carried on the torch of the conversations, and Sufi Monk was just the opposite. Each time we would visit, we'd leave something behind—(not on purpose), or, they'd give us something to take with us.

As I continue sitting on this hard rock, watching the waves lulling themselves to a well-earned rest, I also wonder: Could I possibly mend my ways by being more like Sufi Monk, while keeping the thoughtful gardening patterns that Earthly Rose taught me vicariously while helping heal hundreds of people we know from too much worry in their brains?

We each discover our own dichotomies of being as we age in the era of non-aging, of excess information on our hands that we know not what to with—yet, of all the books and music we learn from, arts and crafts, culinary delights, trips across seas and towns—the surprisingly delightful finds are when we realize who we truly are, and why we exist in our capacities. Can we quieten the chatters inside our minds as Sufi Monk does, no matter what is surrounding us all in this busy hubbub, just to accept what is, rather than complain about what is not? This is what I want to do for me next phase—to silence the chattering brain—to refrain from entertaining myself too much of the world's commodities and chatter, and allow myself the extravagance of silence. That state of being—Sufi Monk's and Earthly Rose, and our generous neighbors—as I see it, can only come from giving up the most cumbersome commodity of all, nearly impossible a feat for most people: excess pride.

Closing Thoughts for Readers

Twelve Pink Roses came into being as a direct result of the twelve roses that sprung up outside my writer's window from God's mercy and grace. A previous Asian family had lived in this garden and planted seeds that now bloom near us. In the back of my mind, I may also have been thinking of the *twelve tribes of Israel that God mentions in the three Revelations.* These are tribes that should revere one another and not fear one another through nationalistic and tribal fragmentation that lead to violence. The poems and vignettes that are included—both mine and my Aunt Nuzhat's—and reflect the *desire to unite people* not through fright but through understanding of one another's similarities and differences alike. We feel and sense the loss of sacred human life everywhere as much as we feel our love for our Maker and all the blessed humanity with diversity, which He has given us to cherish from a distance while making peace with ourselves and God. In between writings, trips, and viewings of societal changes, I would occasionally see a jubilant redbird, and take its picture with much joy in my heart in times of sorrow. Those poems are also included with vignettes from Life's University.

About the Author

Kausam Reza Salam, or Dr. K. (called by her hardworking students), writes because she needs to write as much as she needs to breathe, pray, eat, and speak. Writing has been a lifeline back to the Almighty when life has been rough. She enjoys family and wishes she knew external gardening. She loves her children and her husband deeply even in their toughest times as they evolve through their select professions and faith. She also loves her Global Islamic Ummah of Democracy (GIUD) *deeply* even when nations choose not to get along; she equally loves her new Catholic community, which has taught her how to have faith in humanity's goodness again and hired her, knowing she has had traumas. She also thanks her Islamic school in Houston for *allowing her to be herself* even after traumas. She especially thanks her blessed parents and in-law parents; elders; grandfather, poet, and police officer of justice; grandfather and prime minister of Bihar of justice; loving aunts and uncles; and extended cousins *who practice justice for all*, without whom she would have a harder time surviving these political crises. Kausam appreciates *all her true friends* and true enemies who taught her how to be true to herself despite life's double-edged turmoils, which led her back to inner composure.

Lightning Source UK Ltd.
Milton Keynes UK
UKHW030754240123
415868UK00001B/66